"Jess Janz has a gift: She makes you remember what it feels like to be human. These pages are alive with honesty, courage, and the kind of connection we are starving for in a lonely world. *The Table Where We Meet* is a reminder that meaning is built in the small moments, and every person we meet could change us for the better. Jess captures these truths masterfully."

—Doug Cartwright, founder of
Alchemy Sales Coaching, speaker,
and author of *Holy Sh!t We're Alive*

"In a world that has trained us to lead with our job titles, Jess Janz reminds us that the most revolutionary act is asking someone who they actually are. Drawing from her years of experience convening connection-hungry strangers, she teaches us how to find the courage we need to truly see and be seen by others. *The Table Where We Meet* isn't a book about wishing for connection—it's a road map for practicing it. This book is warm and humorous and insistent that we're all carrying universes inside us that almost no one thinks to ask about. An indispensable book for an age of loneliness."

—Jonathan Merritt, author of *Learning
to Speak God from Scratch*

"When was the last time you lingered over a meal and felt not only satiated but seen? In *The Table Where We Meet*, Jess Janz invites us to sit down and remember what it feels like to be included, welcomed, and wanted. Janz stirs together the perfect balance of self-deprecating humor, heart, and honesty, and the result is feast. Loneliness is the epidemic of our age, but Janz shows us the medicine we most need might just be as simple as showing up for dinner. Compelling, human, and utterly amusing, Janz's debut is one you will not want to miss."

—K. J. Ramsey, licensed therapist and
author of *The Place Between Our Pains:
A Memoir of What Joy Can Survive*

"Required reading for anyone desperate for something real. *The Table Where We Meet* is a guide to soulful conversation, a compelling case for the power of letting yourself be seen, and a roar of hope all in one. If you are sick of small talk, screens, and surface-level living, read this."

—Victoria Hutchins, yoga teacher,
poet, and author of *Make Believe*

"A refreshing, aching portrayal of the human condition and the art of belonging, *The Table Where We Meet* eats and leaves no crumbs."

—Lyndsay Rush, *USA Today* bestselling
author of *A Bit Much*

the table where we meet

LESSONS LEARNED FROM DINNER WITH 1000 STRANGERS

jess janz

Published by Sourcebooks
1935 Brookdale RD, Naperville, IL 60563-2773
(630) 961-3900
sourcebooks.com

Cataloging-in-Publication Data is on file with the Library of Congress.

Printed and bound in the United States of America.
VP 10 9 8 7 6 5 4 3 2 1

To everyone who's met me at the table

...and especially to Ryan.

Table of Contents

Introduction

Setting the Table

Technically, by social standards, I'm *bad* at meeting people.

Secretly, I'm immediately wondering *everything* about them. And social norms would suggest that I shouldn't lead with "Hey, really quick, can you just tell me how you came to be and what you care most about and what's been ruminating nonstop in your mind lately and what's been buoying you during these ridiculous times, and maybe could you also share what you know to be most true?" But I want presence and I want us to say something honest. If we're here, and we're talking, I want there to be an intersection of my world and theirs.

I have always been fascinated by the fact that within each of us is a universe unto ourselves.

It happens in the most common places: Maybe I'm on the bus,

or I'm in line getting coffee, and suddenly I am acutely aware of the humanity woven all around me—each person on this bus, in this coffee line, holds within them unending multitudes of preferences and disappointments, full of all the things they've done and what's happened to them. All this shapes their understanding of who they are and how they show up in the world.

They have a certain dessert they can't resist when they see it on a menu. They might have a specific brand of gum they like (if they're like my mother, original Trident with the paper wrapping). Maybe their ears get hot if someone even suggests they might be a *cat person*. Perhaps one summer they broke their arm. They might have heard the worst news of their life today. They probably have, like all of us tend to have, one or more things they keep in the unsayable place: that thing that is either too precious or too heavy to talk about. And here we all are, pretending we're not all walking miracles. Here we are, sitting quietly next to them on this bus, standing silently behind them in this line, pretending that we have better things to do than find out everything that makes them up.

I've spent a lot of my life wondering if people feel the way I do—if people are curious in the way I am curious, if they are lonely in the way I often feel lonely, especially in conversations that stay in the safe surfacey place. I've been on the lookout for people with whom I can have the kinds of conversations where it feels like we're answering questions as ourselves and not as the version of ourselves that is *fun at parties.*

In this way, the story of Dinner With Strangers starts all the way back when I was an artsy, broody kid with an ocean of feelings who was trying to make sense of the world, who grew up to be, for a time, an aspiring musician in my twenties, writing melancholy folk songs and playing them in sticky bars for the same twelve friends who mercifully kept paying five bucks per show to come see me perform. This meant that I worked in restaurants and retail for most of my adult life, which meant my job title always felt at odds with *what I did*.

It starts with a deep aversion to small talk. It starts with the communal longing to be understood, or the overwhelming desire to start every conversation with *how does it feel to be you?*

It starts in the salon chair of a kitschy hair studio in the east end of Toronto, so hipster that you can't even google it; you just have to know how to get a hold of Ryan.

It starts with a really bad haircut.

Desperate to fix my hair—chunky, brassy streaks and brutalist-style layers that I did *not* ask for that were *not* framing my face in a flattering manner—I made an appointment with a friend's highly recommended hairstylist, Ryan Cantelon (who's been saved in my phone as *Hair Magician* ever since). Ryan fixed me right up, and five hours, ninety million hair foils, and a few toners and potions later, our kindred fate was sealed. We immediately discovered that we both love to talk for hours about what-ifs and what's possible and what we're dreaming about, and that we have a mutual tendency to leap toward a bold, audacious idea if it has even the slightest feeling of being electric and adventurous.

Here's what you'll immediately notice about Ryan: He's as hilarious as he is darling. He's got a kind of magical, ethereal aura around him that makes even the most pragmatic person want to use the word *aura*. The subdued timbre of his voice and mischievous twinkle in his eye only add to his impeccable storytelling; you're enraptured with every meandering turn. He'll take his time, filling in every detail of whatever he's telling you about. He moves through the world at a pace and with a vibrancy that at times make it seem like he's floating. Anyone I've ever met who knows Ryan calls him one of their very dear friends.

I call Ryan the Launcher of Dreams; his hair studio became a place for his friends to start businesses and find their footing. He initially signed the lease with his friend April, a talented designer who was starting a custom wedding dress business. The studio itself was unassuming, on the lower level of a seedy stretch of Queen Street East, sandwiched between a Turkish rug shop and a fishing store. It had craggy stone walls, an industrial barnlike sliding door to the bathroom, stone arched closets that stood at attention in the back of the room, and concrete floors holding layers of stories in the flecks of paint and scratches from so many configurations of different furniture over the years. A thirty-foot fiddle leaf fig tree climbed beside the stair banister, reaching toward the light. The studio was wide and roomy and had a magical energy that was undeniable; anyone could tell upon walking in that beautiful things happened there.

Early into opening the studio, Ryan was talking with a hair client of his, Alex, about what she would do if time and money were not obstacles (a favorite question of his to get people talking about something other than their actual jobs), and her breath caught in her chest and she half-whispered, "Oh, I've always dreamed about opening a flower business. Not even a storefront—I'd love to design florals for weddings and events." Ryan asked what it would take to get started, and while she began with listing all the reasons why she could never pull it off, by the end of the hair appointment, they'd talked through a mock-up of a business plan, a list of equipment she needed to source, and a verbal deal with Ryan that she could start out paying $200 per month to use the studio for the first two months, increasing by $200 for the next few months, until she got her business off the ground. With that, her floral design company was born. In those early days of the studio, clients would walk into their hair appointments surrounded by sheaths of light silk, satin, and lace from April's dresses, and buckets upon buckets of fresh flowers spilling all over the place from Alex.

Dinner With Strangers was also a seed that was planted right there in the studio, first conceptualized during a hair appointment and then planned, launched, and hosted there for a year and a half. It was with Ryan that I started this project that has changed my life.

We hosted our first Dinner With Strangers in May 2017 at a big square table with mismatched dishes and enough food to feed thirty people—for our *eight* guests. Our only rule for the night: No one could say what they did for work. Initially this stemmed from Ryan's personal aversion to listening to any of his clients from the corporate world attempt to unload their workplace dramas onto him during their appointments, and my existential angst around my (lack of) career. Mostly, we found work talk boring and wanted to talk about literally anything else.

What we found out quickly, though, was that by removing work talk—and, with it, the titles we earn, uphold, and often put our self-worth in—we were inviting our guests into a social space with brand-new structures, new ways of introducing ourselves, and new ways of learning how to see each other. Friends with careers that were widely viewed as successful or impressive and who all also find a lot of esteem in what they do—my friend Billy, who took over his dad's business at twenty-eight and quickly turned it into a multimillion-dollar company, or my friend Aliah, who is a literal brain surgeon, or my friend Sam, who does Something Impressive at Something Financial at Something Something money-related place—were challenged at dinner to find ways of talking about their lives, goals, and motivations without mentioning their professional achievements. Likewise, guests who felt as if they were in a professional rut, or didn't put a lot of emphasis on their jobs, or who weren't proud of or satisfied with their work were free to share about the areas of their lives that *did* bring fulfillment and inspiration.

Collectively at the table, we're forced to set aside the subconscious social hierarchy as we share our backgrounds, worldviews, and sources of joy: A stay-at-home mother shares about hoping to make an impact in the world. A CEO shares about feeling like a fraud. A yoga teacher shares about craving more stability. A painter shares about their desire to become more community focused. These are universal struggles and desires regardless of a person's job, and they hold equal weight at the table because we aren't able to ascribe authority or meaning to someone's insights based on their job title.

Ryan and I realized that at each dinner, we were inviting people into an immersive practice of rethinking who we are outside of the titles we give ourselves, and the meaning we give them; to examine what about their life—the things they do and the ways they spend their time and what they find themselves thinking about—they actually attribute to their identity. We were asking people to show up as they are, offer a true, vulnerable part of themselves, and take the time to listen to the person across from them with openness and curiosity.

At the time we started Dinner With Strangers, I was going through one of the worst seasons of my life. At twenty-seven, I was in the abyss of grief from a life-altering trauma; I was aimless as far as having any idea how to make any money from my creative work and, in lieu of that, what professional back-up plan to start working on; I was in angsty not-love love. I was truly having an existential crisis about what I should do next.

The dinners brought deep conversation that felt hopeful and inspiring. I was so relieved to not talk about my serving job or what I should possibly make of my life, while desperately eager to talk about things that were deep and meaningful and true. Hearing other people share about making it through hard times, where they were finding joy, and how they were finding meaning among the mundane buoyed my spirit and began to give shape to a new dream for my future. Ryan and I hosted fifteen grassroots, invite-only, no-tickets-just-bring-a-bottle-of-wine-if-you-want, Crock-Pot-heated, hope-this-tastes-all-right dinners before I took a life sojourn to California to start what I thought would be the rest of my life. That turned into a move back to Toronto with newfound clarity that I wanted to figure out how to turn the dinner series into my job, which was immediately interrupted by a global pandemic that made Dinner With Strangers *not a thing* for three years, which led to officially relaunching the project as a business on my own in September 2023, which inspired one viral TikTok video that catapulted the project into a larger, wilder movement.

It's taken a meandering path to bring Dinner With Strangers where it lands today, but a few elements have been present since day one: the social destabilization of not sharing our job titles and the conversation that is found in its place; the natural closeness that comes with sharing a meal with others; the magic that happens when a group unofficially, communally agrees to share a bit of their stories with each other; and the shocking regularity with which someone you met an hour ago will share a story or an insight that will stick with you for the rest of your life.

Any kind of *measurable data*, any *statistics talk*, is vastly out of character for my usual artsy, floaty mode of operation, but a data point that is measurable is this: I have now had dinner with over one thousand strangers in the last nine years. That's one thousand unique histories and experiences intersecting over a meal. That's one thousand people who were looking for inspiration, connection, a fresh perspective, or a weird social experiment to get themselves out of their comfort zone. That's one thousand testimonies about different ways to go about living a life.

As the person at the helm of these gatherings for the last nine years, I truly feel like my life has become a testament to how we can be irrevocably changed—even saved—by the stories of others. I've heard stories of bravery and stories of triumph, stories about people failing spectacularly, stories about people waking up one day and drastically changing their life, stories about people implementing the smallest changes that have made all the difference, stories about people reinventing themselves over and over, stories about loneliness and disappointment, and I see either myself or a quality I hope to embody in each of them. I see the world from a new vantage point: from where they're sitting at the table.

I've learned a thousand lessons from what people have shared around the table, and after nearly a decade reflecting on what it means to gather and *actually* meet each other, I continue to uncover examples of the roadblocks that keep us from—and the pathways that lead us to—connecting with each other and allowing ourselves to be truly known.

I see it played out at the table constantly that we all mostly want the same things: to find places where we feel like we belong, to foster relationships that offer support and encouragement with people who see us and accept us as we are, and to create lives that have a semblance of fulfillment and meaning. Yet we increasingly find ourselves in a divided and lonely world, siloed to our echo chambers of similar beliefs, hustle-cultured to the brink of burnout and overwhelm, no time or bandwidth for meandering, nuanced conversation or deep, intentional conversation. We are more reachable than ever with social media and cell phones and smartwatches alerting us to every notification, and yet we keep forgetting how to reach for each other.

This book is a testament to our desire to be known and the conditions necessary to cultivate vulnerability, curiosity, and care for those we meet. Even if we're strangers. Even for a moment.

It's a contemplation on the ways we engage each other, and acts as a gentle guide for fostering connection no matter where we find ourselves.

It's a rebuttal to the apathy we're tempted to adopt instead of looking for more ways to take care of our neighbors and communities.

It's a ledger of the goodness in the world—ordinary people with remarkable stories, like Sid teaching us how we can show up for our friends in the simplest ways (even with a morning selfie), Gloria pursuing her dreams of becoming an actor in her fifties, Anne practicing the sacred act of coming out, Jane and Sarah finding through-threads in their stories even though they couldn't be more different from each other, and many others who have gathered at the table to offer their stories of revelation.

It's a love letter to the strangers who've joined me for dinner and sustained me with their humor, wisdom, and compassion.

I hope you'll meet me at the table, stay a while, and leave our time together feeling nourished.

1

We Can't Meet Each Other if We Don't Introduce Ourselves

The Power of a Vulnerable Introduction

For my whole life, I pretty much always have an internal meltdown every time I meet a new person.

"So, Jess, tell me about yourself," they say. Where do I start with *that*? Surely they don't mean for me to answer, as accurately as possible, with all the nuances and intricacies of who I am, and share what activities, experiences, and values I have that help me define my identity. They're simply looking for a few factoids to get the ball rolling on this conversation. They might not even be doing that; they might be filling time with what they think is a very softball, basic question (as if *who are you?* is the most softball, basic question to answer—yeah, right).

And for these reasons, I am calling myself back from the abyss of my existential angst whenever I am in a social situation.

When we first meet someone, we're trying to gather some preliminary information, trying to place each other and create the skeleton structure of who that person is, meaning-making creatures that we are. The intention, more than anything, is to maybe make them feel welcomed into the conversation, or to let them know we're curious about them. I'm not sure why I feel the need to *define my entire existence* to a stranger in every initial meeting. So *when* exactly do we *actually* meet?

Picture it: I'm twenty-one, working as a server at a steakhouse in the Financial District in downtown Toronto. I serve many people in suits, very much part of the song and dance of their business deals and client wooing and *let me subtly show you who's the boss by selecting an impressive bottle of wine and knowing exactly what to order and nonchalantly picking up the bill.* I quickly learn how to read whether a table wants me to be chatty or subdued, ultra-professional or a bit sassy. I have a role to play, and it changes with each group that sits down.

The facade of our little theatrical production will sometimes crumble at the very last minute: Mr. Big Boss Guy is putting his credit card PIN into the machine while I stand respectfully to the side. We're waiting on technology to process the payment, and Mr. Big Boss Guy will ask, "So, what do you do when you're not serving?" I'm an aspiring musician, paying my rent with tips, and I've learned quickly that people in suits whom I serve at this steakhouse have *opinions* about my creative pursuits. I share that I'm a musician and brace for whatever response he might rally back.

He is most likely just making conversation while this forty-five-second transaction completes. He is maybe wondering if the gratuity he just punched into the credit card machine is going toward my education or a night of margaritas. He is perhaps genuinely curious about my life.

He might say, *Oh, do you have an album?* or *Wow! How do you plan on making money from that?* with either curiosity or judgment. I make the assumption that maybe he's a dad who definitely expects his kids to go to university, to have a road map, to believe that their success is imminent and they know where it's coming from. Because I don't have an album and I have made approximately zero dollars from my music career, I get flustered, or I get defensive. I don't have the language or the confidence or the awareness to say to Mr. Big Boss Guy that I just know that I am a Creative, and I'm figuring out what shape that's going to take, and whether or not I'll be able to make a career from the art that I make, but I'm going to make it anyway. Sometimes Mr. Big Boss Guy will be amazed that I say I'm a musician. Or he will be patronizing but will try to be polite with a too-high-pitched *Well, good for you!* Sometimes he won't realize that he's not keeping his judgmental face to himself, and I will take on this stranger's concern or judgment or confusion as a mantle of how *I* should feel about the work I feel called to and the life I am carving out for myself. And then this will repeat at five to twenty tables every night of every shift for years and years of my life.

My friend Nora offers me a revelation as I lament my daily song and dance with patrons. She says, "What if you just…lie?

What if you tell them you're in school for communications or something? Say you're doing something they'd deem 'acceptable' that is clear and 'normal' enough that they probably won't ask follow-up questions, and you will save yourself from feeling like you have to explain or defend yourself a dozen times a night when they're not even asking you to do that."

And thus, my server alter ego is born. The way I introduce myself becomes a party line that protects my hurricane of a heart, instead of a window into who I am. It becomes a tool I employ, which is necessary in the *going about my day* of it all but also has its consequences. By protecting my inner tumultuousness, I'm also preventing that person from knowing who I am, what I care about, what my life is actually like—I am cutting us both off from the possibility of connecting on what's true and meaningful.

I'm walking onto the ferry at Horseshoe Bay in Vancouver to spend a couple of days at my friend Amanda's cute cabin on the Sunshine Coast. She's asked me to swing by her Vancouver apartment and grab her neon-orange Le Creuset Dutch oven so she can make us fresh bread for the weekend, to which I happily oblige (when someone suggests making fresh bread, that's always going to be a yes from me). The gimmick of the large cast-iron pot acts as a portal to connection. Everyone on the ferry has a comment to make at the simple spectacle: "You serving chili?" "What's for dinner?" "Did you save some for me?!" I've never been approached so much in my life and wonder if I've been maneuvering through the world in the wrong way. Is some mildly novel accessory the answer to approachability? Maybe I should become a wacky-hat person. Maybe I should become someone who wears brooches.

One time, still in the serious lockdown days of the pandemic, my boyfriend at the time, Brian, meets me in my neighborhood, armed with cans of cider in Koozies, and we weave through the side streets of the usual route I've been taking for my stupid daily afternoon mental health walk sipping on our afternoon drinks. Usually, these walks are my only source of any human interaction, and out of courtesy, everyone crosses to the other side of the street as soon as they see me coming. It's a new way of caring for each other: giving an extra-wide berth. With it, a new kind of loneliness seeps into my bones, a longing for anyone to reach out in any way (even a nod of acknowledgment would've carried me for days). As I'm now on this walk with Brian, we pass the same houses and the same neighbors I pass each day, and suddenly everyone has something to say about our technically-breaking-the-law beverages, shouting, "You guys have the right idea!" and "I'll join you in a second!" and "I wish I'd thought of that!" and "Pass me a drink!"

I wonder (in half-lament) if it's the silly prop of a cider that gives people an excuse to break the fake social barrier of saying hi to me, suddenly making me not invisible, or if people need something silly and safe and surfacey to chitchat about. Brian suggests that maybe people don't know whether to say hi to a woman who is walking on her own, out of respect, to signal *you are safe, I won't bother you*, and having the buffer of another person makes it clear that everyone's being folksy and neighborly. I think about all the times someone has walked too close to me, all the commutes that have felt unsafe and made me wary, and all the precautions I've taken while walking home in other settings that make the conclusion of his observation necessary, or at least appreciated. I wonder further if there's a way for us to signal to the world that hi, hello, we'd like to be greeted like humans. I consider that maybe the onus is on me to look for the proverbial ciders-in-Koozies, the neon-orange pots to start the conversation with those around me.

———

I'm at an album release party for an artist I don't know at a bar I don't know in Toronto's Corktown neighborhood. The bar is slammed, and I'm standing in more-of-a-chaotic-blob-than-a-line to get a drink. An objectively good-looking man, to whom I happen to not be attracted, nudges me and says, "Hey, want to team up? If you catch a bartender's eye, you order for me, and I'll do the same." The subtext of the social situation is that he is perhaps hitting on me, or at least perhaps opening the door for the possibility of hitting on me. Because of my subjective lack of attraction to him, I wonder what the "right" move is here. Is it rude to engage at all if I assume he might be into me and I am decidedly not into him? I decide that we are humans on this planet, we are humans in this more-of-a-blob-than-a-line together, and we can converse for this brief moment that the universe has brought us together.

Further, I am the can-we-share-in-any-manner-of-ways-what-our-human-existence-is-like person, and the don't-start-any-introduction-with-talking-about-work person, so I conclude that we can talk about not-work for the duration of our brief communal beverage-seeking mission. I ask, "So what's been keeping you busy lately?" and he's a bit taken aback, saying, "Oh, wow…I, um…I've been really getting back into photography lately." "Oh cool!" I reply. "What kind of photography are you into?" He tells me a bit about liking angles and lines and buildings until it's our turn to order from the bartender. I tell him it was nice chatting and to have a great night, and I resubmerge into the crowd, fingers spidering the necks of beer bottles that I'm delivering to my friends.

The guy from the bar loops around a bit later, and then loops around again, saying he really enjoyed talking to me and that he "should really get" my number "so we can talk more over dinner." I tell him, "Thank you so much for asking" (he didn't ask, more insisted that I give him my number, but this is not a time for semantics or technicalities), "but I'm not interested." He is shocked at my response. "But…we had a *moment*," he says. I wonder again if I'm at fault in some way for talking to him at all, but what was the alternative? Because I'm not attracted to him, I should cold-shoulder him, ignore him completely? Is conversing really that transactional? I tell him again that it was nice to meet him and that I wish him all the best, and head outside to call an Uber.

I debrief this interaction with my friend Chris, asking his opinion on if I was being socially irresponsible by…what was my offense?…*engaging in conversation,* and engaging in a way that was mildly, though genuinely, inquisitive about this guy's interests. Chris generously offers, "People *are* used to that kind of transactional interaction. It *is* the social norm to completely shut someone down from talking to you at all if you're not attracted to them. But who wants to live in a world like that?! You're being countercultural, and thank god for that. We need more yous out there, blowing people's minds with casual interactions at album releases." I wonder out loud why it felt like I'd crossed a line, very aware that this guy *felt something between us,* and then felt misled—*led on,* as it were—by me.

"Listen," Chris says in his usual no-nonsense-cut-the-crap way, "he *did* feel something! He felt your awesomeness. He talked about his real life late at night with a stranger in a social situation. He felt something *real* in the middle of a crowded bar where mostly not much is felt. We're not used to that. And if you're going to continue to show up in the world like this, which is the ethos of your entire work and who you are, it's going to require constant, though minor, redirects for people who don't know what it's like to often connect with people in real ways. You just say, 'Yeah, we did *have a moment*—a human moment. And it was great! Thank you for letting me get to know you.'"

⸺

This is a book about meeting each other, but it is not a rule book for *how* to go about that; there is not any one "correct" way. I reserve the right to make up an entire life when it seems appropriate, à la

Mr. Big Boss Guy. I challenge myself to not ask what someone does for work when I first meet them, and if someone says, "So, Jess, tell me about yourself," I usually ask them to get more specific if they don't want a list of hilariously obscure anecdotes or a really intense potential overshare. I am grateful for the novel gimmicks like neon-orange pots on ferries and cider cans on neighborhood walks that give us an easy doorway to connecting, and I want to push myself to strike up conversation while out in the world, admitting that often I am too preoccupied in my own inner world to consider whether I look approachable to anyone I'm passing or sitting beside. I challenge myself to connect in real, meaningful ways, even at loud bars sometimes, and go back and forth on the efficacy of this approach.

I get to assess, to the best of my ability, whether the person asking me about my life is just trying to make light conversation or if they're genuinely curious about who I am, what I care about, and how I'm doing. And it's up to me whether or not, or to what extent, I'm going to offer them a real picture of where they find me. *And,* regardless of their initial intention with these introductory questions, I have the option of going deeper and offering them a bit more insight, if I care to test the waters and see if they'd like to venture out with me.

I am now in the official business of inviting people to examine and practice—and change, maybe!—different ways to introduce themselves. At Dinner With Strangers, instead of starting with the titles of categories we might slot ourselves into (and, by doing so, attempting to *define* ourselves), I ask questions that unlock stories that are easy to recall: a highlight from the week, the "thing" we find ourselves recommending the most (be it a book or a podcast or a brand of socks). We talk about a moment we'd like to freeze in time if we could. We talk about times in our lives we've changed our minds. People leave dinner and I don't know their job title, but I can describe their demeanor, and recall something that is important to them, and say what they're looking forward to in the coming months. Sometimes I run into people from dinner *in the real world* and I'm surprised at where our paths cross—sitting next to each other in a restaurant or going to the same drop-in spin class or seeing them emerge from the subway dressed professionally and conservatively when they were so funky and fashionable and expressive at dinner.

When we choose to hear the subtext of almost any question as "Would you like to share a bit about who you are?" we start to realize that introductions aren't just about merely making sense of each other, categorizing each other in our own personal sorting methods of *successful person* or *interesting person* or *underachieving person* or *eccentric person*. When we ask someone, "What do you do [for work / for fun / on days off / on Tuesdays]?" we are really asking, "Can you tell me a little bit about who you are / what you care about / what lights you up / what made you laugh this week / what you do to cheer yourself up / anything you love?" So whether we decide that these more inquisitive questions are implied, or someone is aware enough, present enough, and vulnerable enough to ask them outright, we're invited to share something true about ourselves, and by doing so, we are opening ourselves up to be known.

2

"What's Your Favorite Movie?" and Other Terrible Questions

Engage in Meaningful Ways

Rick is dressed like a TV chaplain. Or maybe he's dressed like the chaplain they base TV chaplains on: He's wearing a collared, checkered shirt under his crimson sweater, wire-framed glasses in front of his kind eyes, loafers, a badge that says *volunteer clergy* around his neck. His gentle disposition, or maybe the softness of his sweater, or maybe the softness of the present moment in my Aunt Mimi's hospital room in the ICU makes my mom and me quickly answer yes when he asks if he can pray for us. Though my relationship with The Church is thorny at best, my relationship with reaching for what is sacred is easy: My hands are wide open.

Mimi was the fifth member of my nuclear family: She was as seamlessly a part of our crew as my mom, dad, sister, and I are. Eleven years older than Mum, she was in her mid-thirties and single when Mum was twenty-three and pregnant with me (and with my six-month-old sister already in tow). When Mimi heard the news that I was on the way, she responded, "It's going to be *really* bad for like two years, and then you'll be young and they'll be old and someday you'll sleep again. It's going to be great." In those early years, she drove from her home in Seattle, Washington, to stay with us in Langley, British Columbia, nearly every weekend, helping with nap time and playtime and diapers and dinner, and I'm sure her presence was the single thing responsible for Mum's last thread of sanity staying intact on most days.

She was a fixture at birthdays and dance recitals and Easter, sleeping over the whole week before Christmas, and sending glittery snail mail in lavender-colored envelopes in the weeks in between. Over the years she became a confidant for me, distinct from the close relationship I have with my parents: one degree removed from the intensity of parenthood but a pillar of influence nonetheless. She was a different entity in my life altogether. She was simply my Mimi, a noun unto itself: keeper of my secrets, a creator of magic for all of us, our softest landing place, our most loyal companion.

I could tell something was wrong in late November 2022 when I had multiple missed calls and *when will you be home and available to talk?* texts from Mum. When I called her back, she said she'd driven down to Washington after Mimi stopped responding to texts and found her collapsed on the floor of her apartment after having had a diabetic seizure and a stroke. She was now in the ICU, in a medically induced coma, and on life support.

I did the thing you do when you get news like that: I canceled everything and got on a plane to Seattle.

So here we are, standing beside her hospital bed, staring at Chaplain Rick, saying yes to a prayer that may or may not make any kind of difference other than to possibly bring some comfort.

Chaplain Rick asks if she's married. We say no. He asks if she has kids. My body slams against the question like the waves of the Pacific thrash against the coast that raised me, refusing to settle. I'm not her daughter, but I *belong* to her; how do I explain that nuance in this impossible moment? She never married, but that doesn't mean she hasn't loved deeply or hasn't had an entire history of love and loving.

The statistics that we use to measure *who we are* hardly encompass anything about a life.

What it comes down to is that Chaplain Rick's questions were tragically inadequate (bless him, he was just doing his well-intentioned rounds). And though benevolent in gathering this preliminary information about my aunt, he missed an opportunity to learn anything about her.

Imagine if he'd asked instead, "Who are the people who are most important to her? Who are the people who would grieve for her?" He would've gotten a completely different answer—and a much fuller picture of who Mimi was, the people she loved, and those who loved her right back.

I think we ask the wrong questions all the time. And in doing so, we miss responses that would lead to deeper conversation—which would lead to *actually* meeting each other. We come by it honestly; we are busy and tired and generally just fumbling along not even sure what we actually want to know. We are well-meaning with our inquiries, looking for a starting point in conversation and genuinely trying to learn about the other person, but the questions we choose can often hold us back from what we're hoping to achieve.

It's easy to get stuck in conversational dead ends when we ask topical questions that leave out stories, specifics, or room for reflection. For example, two things happen whenever people ask me, "What's your favorite movie of all time?" First, I immediately forget every title of every movie I've ever seen; no movie title exists in the history of any information that's ever entered my brain. Second, once the initial amnesia wears off, I then get really in my head about *what it says about me* if I answer with an artsy movie or a rom-com or an intellectual movie or a cult classic. Furthermore, what constitutes a favorite movie? One that's heartwarming? The one I've seen the most or that feels the most nostalgic? One that really moved me or made me think? Each of those quantifiers results in a different answer. And even within each quantifier, we are already getting to a better question: Instead of the root of the question being *define yourself to me*, we actually *engage* each other by asking, "What's a heartwarming movie you love?" or "What movie really made you think?" or "What nostalgic movie do you love?" Those get us talking about optimism, thought provocation, and nostalgia.

I've learned at Dinner With Strangers that the best kinds of questions get people sharing the singular and the specific. They get people telling a story, and from the story, we'll not only learn something about the storyteller, but we'll also feel more connected after the telling of the story. Even if we're on the topic of movies, I don't want someone to list off a movie title; I want to know *why* a certain movie moved them, why it might be in their roster of favorites. I want to know what part most made them laugh. I want to know how it relates to their story, if at all, or if it inspired them in some specific way. I want to know if they used to watch it with their cousins whenever they visited, or if it was the first movie they ever saw in a theater. I want to know which monologues they've memorized, or which character's fashion style they copied after watching it. I want to know which movies made them believe in love, or believe in leaving. I want to know which movies unlocked a portal to a new way of living, and what changes came after seeing it.

In 2018 I move to San Francisco and leave behind my music, my creative community, my weird monthly dinner series at Ryan's hair studio that I started the year before. There's no longer any time for my daily musings on my blog. Despite my lack of transferable skills, I get a job as an executive assistant to a tech billionaire (which is a very fun sentence to say at parties; it has *shock value*). Meanwhile, I stop calling myself an artist, to strangers and to myself. I have health insurance, a salary, vacation days. And I feel like I've been gutted out like a fish. When I have to introduce myself, I wrestle with the desire to tell people everything I *used* to do in my former life, to offer up some evidence that I used to have passions and interests before my whole life became answering emails and changing travel itineraries in the middle of the night. I want to talk about anything other than jobs or bosses or seed-round funding.

I'm out at a pub with my boyfriend Andrew's tech friends, sitting at a long table in the back with a Texas flag and a huge painting of Gandhi above our heads. The tech friends are so nice, making a solid effort to make me feel included and ask me lots of questions. We are yelling over the loud pop playlist blaring over the speakers.

"SO, JESS, ARE YOU JUST LOVING SAN FRANCISCO SO FAR?" Elga asks, her elbows propped up, her face beaming at me. I do a bit of an inventory of the situation: Is she assuming I'm going to say it's great? Is she open to the nuance of how I'm actually doing, how moving to a new city—a new country, in fact—and changing pretty much everything about my life is a huge adjustment, much more than I was anticipating? Would I totally kill the vibe if I yelled back, "ACTUALLY, IT'S BEEN MOSTLY OVERWHELMING AND WEIRD AND HARD—BEING ABLE TO WALK TO THE GOLDEN GATE BRIDGE FROM OUR APARTMENT IS LARGELY RESPONSIBLE FOR MY MENTAL SANITY RIGHT NOW, ELGA"? (Probably, yes.)

She's assuming I must be loving the city, this romantic, wild storyline that Andrew and I are living: whirlwind long-distance romance after a meet-cute at a wedding among the redwoods of Santa Cruz, catapulting ourselves into cohabitating in a (new for me) city after eight short months. Her question is leading the witness, your honor; how could I tell her anything otherwise?

We do this all the time: forget to make room for someone to answer us—to tell us, for themselves, what their experience of any one thing has been. Instead, we project what we think they're feeling right into the way we phrase our questions. I continue to catch myself in the way I phrase the questions I ask people, to let them tell me about their experience instead of ever phrasing anything with "That must have been [fill in the blank: amazing / thrilling / hard for you / exciting / the best upbringing ever / the coolest place to live]."

I still get this wrong. Just recently, I meet my good friend Jason's sister, Krista, for the first time. We're at their childhood friend Josh's concert, and Krista's reminiscing about how Jason and their other four siblings would sneak her into venues to see Josh play when she was a teenager. I proclaim, "That must have been *so fun* to have so many older siblings taking you around and showing you the ropes!" And she quickly corrects me graciously, saying, "Well, yeah, but mostly I just felt left behind. They were all already living their lives and busy with their grown-up decisions and grown-up milestones and I was just the youngest one, which means being mostly overlooked, bored at home." I course-correct, grateful for this gentle reminder from Krista, whether she realizes what she invited me into or not. I've projected my own assumptions instead of letting her tell me what it was like for her. Now I ask her what it was like growing up in a house with four siblings, when and how she found her own path, whether anyone takes her seriously yet, how often she still has to remind them she's not a baby anymore but a thirty-something squarely in adulthood. By letting her tell me about herself, I get to know a bit about where she comes from and what she's like, her eyes crinkling in the corners with a sweet mischief and softness, exactly like her brother's do when he's telling me a story about the people he loves.

My nephew, Gus, is born four months after Mimi died. For ten years before his arrival, my sister and brother-in-law waited and prayed. They mourned the loss of six pregnancies before him. For those ten years, people often asked my sister when she was finally going to have kids.

After each loss, people would often say something like, "Don't worry; you'll have a baby someday!" as if this might make the loss obsolete. They wouldn't ask what her relationship to hope is, given her experience with loss, and with examining what it means to create a life full of meaning in the midst of wishing for something else. People were quick to comfort, but they were also quick to try to make it better, instead of asking what it has been like for her.

And then, for nine months, people often remarked that she *must be so excited* and forgot again to ask, "How are you feeling?" or "What kind of anxieties are coming up for you?" And of course, my sister was thrilled during her pregnancy with Gus—along with carrying a learned hesitancy to get her hopes up. With each week that Gus continued to grow inside her, the stakes grew too. Every week, it felt like there was more to lose.

Our family structure begins to model the one we grew up with; I don't think I'll have kids, but I love being an aunt. Strangers often ask me what Chaplain Rick asked about Mimi—am I married, do I have kids. When I sprained my ankle last spring and hobbled around my Little Portugal neighborhood in a moon boot, three different tiny grandmothers stopped me in the span of a single block, took both my hands, and asked with deep concern, "What happened to you?! Where is your husband?! He should carry your groceries!" Every once in a while, someone will stick me with a "You seem so great! How is it *possible* that you're still single?!" The framework of this question always baffles me. It suggests that a relationship is our reward for being a great person and also comes off as if, because I *seem* so great *and yet* I'm single, there must be something secretly wrong with me.

It's possible to "still" be single for eight million reasons, up to and including the fact that great love is rare, and the alchemy of two people being in the same place at the same time is even more rare. I'm not talking about the location and logistics of stumbling into the same restaurant at the same time; I'm talking about being open and ready and present enough to become aware of each other, and to be brave and willing enough to embark together.

People ask why I'm single, but I wish they'd ask me what I'm learning about love lately instead.

Gus calls me Gigi, a special name that belongs to just us. Have you ever had a twinkly-eyed fifteen-month-old call for you for the first time? *That,* my friends, will recalibrate your brain chemistry permanently. I write on postcards every time I visit a new city and collect them to give to Gus in a few years to show him where I've taken my love for him with me.

On the day my niece (Gus's sister!), Lucy, is born, I'm flying home from Ecuador, and the airport only has those cheesy nature photography postcards available. I buy two postcards this time, one with two turtles and one with a gaggle of long-necked tropical birds. I write on Gus's, "I swam with turtles on this trip! I watched the pelicans eat breakfast on my runs each morning!" and, on Lucy's, "Welcome to the world! Here you are!"

I board my plane and sit next to a young man who is quick to ask me about my travels, saying he'd love to practice his English with a Canadian. He's the first to hear about Lucy's arrival forty minutes ago. I'd seen him at the front of the security entrance, bending his towering six-foot-four frame to hug a tiny woman with the same-shaped chin as him, both of them crying softly. She reached up to wipe the tears from his still-boyish cheeks. On the plane he tells me that he's just been home for the first time since going to school in Brazil two years ago and is now heading back there for another year or so before he'll see his family again.

"Your first time in Ecuador?!" he says, his face lighting up at the news. "Tell me, how did my country welcome you? What will you tell your friends about your time here?"

"What a great question," I say, smiling. I turn to face him and tell him my favorite stories from the last three weeks, hoping he can hear how much this time in his country inspired me while I found the words to write this book.

3

i Hate to Admit That Small Talk Might Have a Place (i Doubt it, Though)

There Are Many Routes to the Deep End

It's August 2024. I'm hosting Dinner With Strangers at my childhood friend Philip's swanky, cool, trendy loft in Brooklyn, New York, and my internet friend Toussaint sends me a text to let me know he's taking the train out from Minneapolis so he can attend.

Of course, an Internet Friend is someone you come across online and develop a friendship with via memes and voice notes and comments made on each other's work despite never (or not as of yet) meeting in real life—a welcomed modern marvel of the twenty-first century in the midst of the otherwise often-a-hellscape that is the digital age. I'm thrilled at the news, both to get to meet Toussaint in the real world and to have at least one guaranteed guest who I know will be a shoo-in for great insights, stories, and thoughtful conversation.

This is my second dinner at Philip's this year, and my second time working with his longtime kindred friend Danielle, a certified Beautiful Human Being and an incredible chef—though she may fight me on claiming the title of *chef,* saying she's not *serious enough* or *professional enough* or something silly like that, even as she rolls out homemade dough for the turkey potpies she's making from scratch. She and her husband, Gordon (also a certified BHB and an insanely talented photographer and visual storyteller), live upstate in a darling farmhouse in the middle of a lavender field. They've agreed to partner with me on these Brooklyn dinners, bringing them to life with their creativity and thoughtfulness and talent infused in every element of the evening, from the menu to the wines chosen to the table decor and everything in between.

The table is overflowing with zucchini and blackberry salad, fresh burrata with fat cherry tomatoes doused in golden olive oil and flaky salt, wood-plank-roasted salmon garnished with dill, and risotto with wild mushrooms and shallots, and all the produce came straight from Danielle and Gordon's garden. Toussaint joins the other guests at the grazing table over briny olives and chunky slices of sourdough with slow-churned chive butter, sipping on tart cocktails. Our ice cubes have bright-orange poppies frozen into them. Once all nine guests arrive, we jump right into the pile of "icebreaker" question cards I've placed next to the whipped ricotta spread.

Toussaint reads out the first question: *What's something that makes you lose all track of time?* Like any icebreaker exercise, this is by no means supposed to be a question that stumps anybody or makes anyone think too hard about their response. Toussaint, however, immediately shakes his head and says, "Damn, Jess, really getting us *right* into it here!!!" I'm surprised that he's so taken aback, knowing him to not shy away from The Deep Stuff, having had very intense conversations with him throughout the year about serious, heavy, hard topics.

I tease, "These are supposed to be the *softball* questions, Toussaint! If you're already overwhelmed, then you're in trouble when we sit down at the table!" He searches for his words and shares something about losing track of time when he's playing music. He passes the proverbial conversation baton to the next person.

Eventually moving to the dinner table and settling into the main course, we all weave deeper into our conversation. Margot shares about her current relationship, and how, with her current partner, she sometimes has difficulty knowing or trusting if this is the right relationship for her because their dynamic is peaceful, supportive, and drama-free. She wonders aloud if their relationship is therefore missing the tumultuousness of chaos that other relationships have had in the past that we can so often misconstrue for *passion*, for *chemistry*, for *kismet*. We all nod in recognition—we are evidently a table full of people who feel most alive when in the muck.

Toussaint leans back, *mmms* and *aahs* a bit at Margot's story, lets out a big sigh, and then says, "So earlier, when that very first question came up, I thought it was too early to get right into this. I talked about my love for music, but the truer answer is that I lose all track of time—and feel the most myself—in the middle of a seri-ous crisis. I'm the one who everyone calls when the worst happens: when an encampment of people who are unhoused gets evicted, or a community member is shot by police, or when someone gets arrested at the protest. I know *exactly* who I am in those moments. I know exactly what to do. I feel so clear and aware and needed. I know what I have to give. I know how to help and what to say and who to call. And I've been wondering at what point am I looking for crisis, am I welcoming it, am I opening the door for the next terrible thing to come knocking, because I feel the most myself and the most helpful when the worst is happening?"

I'm not the one to speak with authority on the topic of avoid-ing chaos and crisis; I am the poster child for both, seeking angst and pining in romantic endeavors, welcoming the strife of the unre-quited and the *not quite right* or the *not quite right now* or the *maybe if the circumstances changed just the smallest bit, in which case I'll cling on and wait around.* Likewise, I feel the most myself when holding hands with the anguish of the world. I don't flinch when people share stories of the ugliest things that happen to us in this lifetime. Put me at a cocktail party where I'm supposed to be light and airy and funny and carefree and make conversation about the weather or city traffic or pop culture for more than four minutes, however, and my internal battery will be absolutely depleted, and I will also ques-tion what's wrong with me that I can't simply make charming, light-hearted conversation and just be happy to be having a nice time.

Toussaint's reflection on his in-crisis flow state, in tandem with the fact that he refrained from initially answering the original icebreaker question by talking about it—and was *able* to refrain until later, which I find impressive and nearly impossible, being the way I am—further makes me wonder whether there is such thing as a "light" or easy question, since a question is only as simple or funny or reflective or intense as the answer that follows. How then are we supposed to determine when is the right time to take a conversation into the deep end?

There was a therapist I worked with for a while with whom I had a cute, ongoing, fake-argument shtick (she would probably call it something different, like *a serious roadblock* or *an inability to see how this is a harmful pattern that is negatively affecting my life*); she and I disagreed about the importance and necessity of small talk, and for how long anyone should continue with it in any given conversation.

Tanya the Therapist's Small Talk Manifesto

1. You can't just launch right into the deep end.
2. It takes time to get to know someone, and it *should* take time to get to know someone.
3. If you share too much, too quickly, the other person may not be ready for that level of intensity; they may be put off and may not open up to you at all, whereas if you give it some time, you may eventually go further and get closer overall.

4. If you're sharing so much of yourself right off the bat, the other person hasn't earned that level of intimacy and vulnerability from you, and hasn't proven that they can safely and respectfully handle the delicate things you've shared with them.

5. Does every interaction and conversation have to *go somewhere?*

My Rebuttal

1. Watch me do a cannonball.

2. If the point is to get to know each other when we interact, why shouldn't we get right to it?

3. Okay, obviously, yes, fine, one point for Tanya. There is a level of conversational consent to make sure we're not emotionally dumping on someone in a conversation that they don't want to be in.

4. At a certain point (an as-of-yet-undetermined length of time), someone should push the vulnerability needle further, no? And is it not an act of vulnerable generosity to offer your own depth to someone?

5. Not every interaction and conversation has to go somewhere, but even a lighthearted exchange can be a point of connection if we just give the smallest ounce of sincerity.

When I'm considering the cadence of questions to ask at any dinner, we of course work up to the *meatier* questions. Starting with lighter conversation allows the group to relax into the night, get rid of initial jitters, and for trust to be subtly, steadily built by way of banter and easy chatter as the group finds and establishes their collective rhythm (perhaps this falls under Tanya the Therapist's argument #3; I'm disgruntled to think that she might be gaining points all over the place). But I'm not sure there's a right (or wrong) or best time for Toussaint to have shared about his role in moments of crisis; he could have shared it right off the bat, and it would have started the night off on a different tone than the one we ended up having because he waited.

I've seen over the years that each group has its own pace with which it heads toward the deep end. In the early days of Dinner With Strangers with Ryan, we would handwrite our questions on scrap paper and divide them into two bowls for the dinner table: "beginner" questions in one bowl and "heavy hitters" in another. We'd have someone draw a question, as opposed to how I run them now: preselecting what questions I'm going to ask the group based on the theme of the night and creating a flow in the conversation instead of leaving it up to chance. At one of our very first dinners, my friend Amir draws the first question from the heavy hitters bowl—"How is your life different from a year ago?"—and he shares that his brother's health has been declining steadily. And while he's witnessed his brother's deteriorating health, he and his sister, with whom he's had a strained relationship for decades, are learning how to reconcile with each other, leaning on each other for support, mourning together, making impossible decisions with care and consideration of each other's opinions. It's a beautiful, harrowing peek into the challenges that Amir is currently facing in his life, and I'm incredibly moved that he's willing to be so vulnerable right off the bat. And because Amir set the tone with his answer, the entire night was filled with really vulnerable reflections from the other eight guests, almost like they were responding in kind and meeting his earnestness with their own.

After one particular dinner at which Hilary shared that she'd lost her husband last year and reflected on some of the challenges of navigating the unimaginable, I get some constructive criticism in the anonymous post-dinner feedback form I send out after each event: Someone shares that they find it really intense that Hilary shared such personal information, and that the topic of grief or death might be triggering for some people and that I'm not creating a safe environment by allowing such topics to come up. Grief indeed is as intense as it gets, but it is an overwhelmingly human experience, which is to say that grief is pretty much inevitable. It's something that we can all relate to in some form or another. Hilary's lived experience is that her husband died, and she felt safe enough to share that at the table. How beautiful that a room of strangers could offer a container for her to share about losing her husband.

When considering this feedback about creating a "safe" environment, I wonder about the difference between protecting people from potentially feeling uncomfortable and creating a space where people feel safe enough to share about the difficult things they're facing, even if those difficult things make the rest of us face our own discomfort with mortality, with grief, with death, or with any other categorically messy or difficult experience that comes with being human. Safety is anchored in the collective gentle handling of these delicate topics—the way we should hold anything precious.

Guided sauna–cold plunge–meditation studios have taken Toronto by storm lately, and I agree to go to a late-afternoon session with a friend after swimming and tanning at the beach all day. We're sun-soaked and floaty heading into this class that is themed "Emotions: A to Z." We move into the massive, expertly lit sauna that is radiating the studio's signature essential oil scent (which is dashed onto a massive, perfectly round ice ball that will be thrown by the instructors in perfect unison on the rocks as soon as class starts; the scent of ylang-ylang opens up the heart channels, in case you didn't know). Within twenty seconds of the session starting, the lights are brought to almost pitch-black and the man leading the meditation is yelling about accessing the anger within us. "Go there! Find your anger! I want everyone on the count of three to yell *FUCK!!!!!* as loud as you can!!!!!" I am jolted from the blissful state of my beach day into a bunch of people in this sweaty room screaming profanities before the oil-doused snowball even had a chance to dissipate.

While I am no stranger to heavy emotions and generally

unafraid to do some internal examination of difficult feelings, the immediate demand to *go there* without any context, introduction, or invitation felt forced, superfluous, and performative. I wonder if the intensity I can lead with or hope to arrive at can feel off-putting to some. I add this to my personal checklist of considerations: Am I metaphorically acting like a glitzy sauna guide with my own agenda, lurching people in a direction they haven't even considered whether or not they want to go?

There are all sorts of routes to reach the deep end: either by catapulting or rowing a boat, by sprinting in without checking our pockets for valuables or wading in inch by inch, by dunking our head quickly or taking care not to get our hair wet. We all have our own preferred method and reasons why we take that approach if we can. As for me, I'm game for the dramatic dash to the center and struggle with the slower approaches, but I know there are merits to each and something to learn from those who approach reaching the depths in opposite ways from me.

Maybe we need each other's different pacing at which we reach the depths; we need people like Toussaint, who are at their best when the unimaginable happens, in the same way that Toussaint needs people around him who encourage him to find levity, or who help him to unwind, or who allow him to show up as he is without needing to contribute something useful.

My dad goes into Full Dad Mode whenever we're en route

somewhere. To be in a parking garage, a mall, an airport with that man is to watch him take off in rocket-launcher pace, leaving us in the dust. First to the car, always. Meet you at the luggage carousel. Mum will sometimes send a photo to the group chat: Each picture is some version of Dad's back at varying distances while they're on a walk "together," with the caption "Nice stroll on the pier!" or "Really loving our afternoon walk." Mostly, we find this trait amusing, but I get annoyed by it occasionally: Why, sir, must you walk so fast? Unless the intention is to run ahead so as to bring the car around in order to get us where we need to go faster, what's the rush? Why not walk together? I am a fast walker myself, and my default mode when running errands or walking to a meeting could be described as turbo speed, and when walking with others, I sometimes realize that they're working hard to keep up with my winding and weaving through sidewalk traffic.

Just because we each have a preference for the way we like to move through the world doesn't mean that everyone needs to, or should, meet us there. There are merits to slowing down, just as there are merits to having someone push us to pick up our feet, find a jog when we'd otherwise shuffle, a quick sprint to push us out of our comfort zone, a marathon when, left to our own devices, we would've quit miles ago, proving to ourselves and to each other that we had it in us all along.

The key is that the pace is set collaboratively, with a collective willingness to adjust throughout the journey.

I think in every interaction we have, whether commenting on

the weather or sharing a funny anecdote about our nephew or leading with divulging that we're having a hard day, we're really saying
to each other, "I'd like to embark in this direction with you; are you
willing to come along, and at what pace do you feel comfortable
going?" Every question we ask each other is an invitation to embark
somewhere together, each with our varying degrees of openness,
readiness, and willingness to share at any given time. When we are
adaptable with our tempo in order to match each other's stride, we
find ourselves in step.

It takes great vulnerability to share anything with each other.

It takes great care to consider how what we share might affect
the listener.

It takes great awareness to see someone sharing anything with
us as a bold offering of connection.

4

Why Do We Ask "How Are You?" if We Don't Mean it?

Greet Each Other Earnestly

I start my first job working as a barista at a coffee shop—I think I'm *so cool* because it isn't a fast-food-chain job like my other high school friends have; no, no, this is a *classy, cool* job. I work with *mostly adults*. I make *lattes*, not *burgers*, okay?

I love the lightning-fast pace of the morning rush, the magical dance while working the bar with someone else, the long slew of orders tag-teamed with proficiency and speed, and the number of people I get to talk to every day. And it is here at this bustling neighborhood coffee shop that I first realize a specific kind of heartbreaking rejection whenever I ask customers, "How are you?" and they respond with an automated, unreflective, one-word *"Finethankyouhowareyou."*

At first, my little sixteen-year-old heart takes it personally when people didn't engage: Do they not want to talk to me? Do they just not want to get into it? Do they not realize how seriously I mean it—that me asking isn't just a formality, that I truly want to know? Or is it that they're so closed off that they don't even *know* how they're doing? Do they not know that I am inviting them into a moment of human connection, even here (*especially* here) at this coffee shop chain in the center of suburbia?

This is not the first time I'll come to feel like I'm taking something way too seriously. It will certainly not be the last. There is definitely the argument here that it's simply *not that deep*; first of all, no one owes anyone any access or insight into their lives at any moment, and it is completely acceptable to not engage when someone tries to strike up a conversation. Also, there isn't actually very much time at all in how long it takes to make a cappuccino to necessarily share even an anecdote about anyone's day, let alone give a remotely meaningful (or, gasp, vulnerable!) answer. Sometimes the time someone has waiting for their coffee is the only four minutes they have to themselves that day, and they don't want to spend that time unpacking their inner feelings to a teenage barista. I get it. AND YET.

To take the world overwhelmingly seriously is what makes me Not Fun at Parties, and it is also the role of the poet: to marvel at a blade of grass, to become fascinated with moments of monotony like waiting in line and where our minds wander while folding laundry, to take a magnifying glass to the simplest things and find their significance.

One time I shared a poem online that I'd written called "All This Love and Loving," which talks about what I've learned from each relationship I've had—one of those lessons being to see "the water glass brought to my side of the bed as a radical act of tenderness." A "troll" of sorts commented on the post, "What's tender about a fucking glass of water?! You don't even know how language works, do you? You can't just make shit up." I thought this comment was incredibly amusing, because poets literally *make stuff up* all the time. The art form itself is free of rules, defiant of them, in fact. Also, to ask a poet "what's so tender" about anything is basically a dare.

In response, I put it out to my online community to retaliate this person's inquiry by writing poems about tender glasses of water, and over sixty people sent me poems, and even more stories and snippets of their lives: glasses of water brought gingerly to broody teens who keep saying they're fine. Straws held to the lips of sick loved ones in their final days. The way someone's husband brought her a glisteningly cold glass of water right after she gave birth to their daughter. Someone working in a restaurant who saw an ex come in with his new wife and brought them both waters after she saw that no one else had done so yet. My Uncle Mike, in his coffee shop–owning days, writing a poem about a kid who never bought anything and seemed to need so much, who would ask for a glass of water but never two. It was our collective defiance against someone saying *get over it, it's not that deep.*

To be a poet (or, more broadly, a creative, or even more broadly, any person who cares to walk gently and inquisitively on this earth) is to insist that everything should, in fact, be examined with tenderhearted scrutiny, including: What does it mean to greet each other? Why do we ask "How are you?" if we don't mean it? What would change about our daily interactions if we did? What if we were able to offer a tiny bit of a real answer when someone asked us? What if we used that interaction as an invitation to open up to each other, even to strangers, even for a brief moment?

Think about the practice and ritual of it: Here we are, acknowledging each other's existence. Here we are, hopefully for a moment looking each other in the eye. Here we are, first order of business, asking about how we find ourselves today. Here we are, missing it over and over again—the opportunity to share a small insight of our humanness with each other.

Here we are in this neighborhood coffee shop in the bleary morning, paths otherwise not crossing, with all sorts of realities and difficulties—me, a teenage barista with deep existential angst about what I'm going to do with my whole life, with a head full of songs and poems that maybe at this stage are really not that great and surviving the super, truly heinous what-a-drag that is high school, nursing my first impossibly broken heart after Hot Steve[1]

---

1 Would you believe me if I told you that I started up a romance with the impossibly unattainable cute guy with the perfect 2000s shaggy beachy-blond hair, who was *actually* an Abercrombie model, whom I'd liked for years and seemed so unattainable that my friend group had such a nickname as *Hot Steve* for him, and that our romance blossomed over Myspace after he started liking my wistful posts and we started Skyping every night, which I could only do via my dad's work laptop because this was pre-everybody-had-their-own-computer, and he'd write me beautiful letters with perfect architecture handwriting on red paper that he sprayed with his cologne???? What a time to be alive.

said he didn't want to write me letters from architecture school in San Diego anymore while he was home over Christmas break. That stuff cuts deep. And yet here I am, *persevering*—here I am brewing coffee and steaming milk despite all my personal melodramas that feel so serious, so that you, perhaps driving your kid to Saturday morning volleyball practice on what would otherwise be the only day you could sleep in all week, can caffeinate on your way, can hold your venti sugar-free vanilla extra-hot nonfat latte close to your body while you nod a silent hello to the other parents in the stands, whom you may or may not ask how their days are going, may or may not ask generally or specifically *how's it going*—"it" being anything at all in their lives, "*it*" being their internal or external world—to which they may or may not answer about schedules or busyness or Kendall's math homework or the teacher-parent meetings next week or their stale marriage or their in-laws coming to visit or the bewilderment that this is what life has become: lattes and car pools and volleyball games and baristas with too many thoughts in their heads. Yes, you standing here in front of me at the counter beside the case of croissants and banana bread, our worlds colliding in this small moment, I am *greeting* you: Hello, welcome to your day. Hello, welcome to this space. How are you? How *are* you? How are *you*?

Maybe part of the problem is that *how are you?* is such a vast and broad question. Are we meant to give a general synopsis of our overall well-being, all things considered, on a scale of one to ten? Our overall physical state, or our mental state? How do we differentiate between the autopilot don't-actually-have-capacity-to-find-out *how are you?* and the do-you-want-to-share-something-about-your-life-with-me *how are you?*

If the rebuttal is that asking "How are you?" is just a formality, that truly *there isn't time for all that,* then maybe we should trade it out for a more accurate question, something more palatable, approachable, a softer starting point. Maybe we could ask what we actually want to know, like "What did you get up to this week?" instead of *"How* was your week?" to show that we want a general overview of activities instead of a potential check-in of each other's emotional state. We could ask about each other's weekend plans if we want to know about weekend plans, and as an added bonus, we'll find out something about the other person's interests, which may or may not overlap with our own interests, which would lead to camaraderie over something we both like, or the opportunity to learn about something new. Someone might have reservations at the restaurant we went to last week. They might be going to the same concert we're going to. They might be getting their first tattoo. And maybe when greeting each other, if there isn't time for any of that, we don't need to ask any question at all; we can welcome each other genuinely and leave it at that.

I do know the other side of this coin: In the hardest season of my life, I found *how are you?* to be the most difficult question to answer—to baristas and close friends alike. It's one of the many ways grief and trauma feel so isolating; it feels impossible to say, "I'm trying to make sense of the world after the unimaginable happened to me." The truth of our reality feels too heavy to impose on others. It also feels so unbearably exposing to share even a snippet of the truth while in a difficult season and have someone not catch what we're saying, or not be able to hold it, and how are we supposed to assess if they can?

I found the antidote to this separate feeling was to share something that felt true, even if it was cloaked; the moments when I was able to say to anyone even something as broad as "It's a weird time right now!" or "I'm having a hard day" or "Life is life-ing real hard right now!" invited people to meet me where I was. And *being met* just means that we are not standing alone holding the impossible thing in that moment.

At a dinner recently, Katy walks into the event space with her bright-blue eyes twinkling. She has the usual buzz of nervousness that guests generally have upon arrival, but our initial conversation flows easily as I get her coat tucked away and get her a drink. I notice that she has a small, fresh tattoo kissing the outside of her wrist that says "boop," which is objectively a cute word, obviously. "What a sweet tattoo!" I say, and she responds softly, "Thank you. I got it in memory of my husband." So much shared in one sentence. Coupled with the freshness of the tattoo, her comment led me to gather that this was a recent loss. "I'm so sorry," I say. "What a sweet way to commemorate your love." We chat a bit, and I tell her, "Take what you need from tonight and only share what you feel comfortable sharing with a room full of strangers—if you don't want to be the person who recently lost her husband for the night, give yourself permission to do that."

Throughout most of the night, Katy does just that: She speaks in generalities, alluding to going through the most difficult season of her life, an unexpected shift in plans, picking herself back up after things didn't go the way she thought, having the rug pulled out from under her.

It strikes me as she shares without divulging the details that we don't have to know the full story in order to see ourselves in each other's stories.

There is a universality to the generalities that Katy is speaking about—do we not all recognize the feeling of the rug pulled out from under us in our own interpretation and experience?

At any given time, someone can be going through the worst season of their life and still, somehow, be a functioning human, let alone a human who, I don't know, gets dressed, puts on mascara, is laughing at someone's joke, is telling a story about something unrelated to the worst thing that's ever happened to them. Here is Katy sharing in generalities about her great loss, followed by a story about something funny that happened in her yoga class, a mishap with mistaking someone's shirt as her own, how could she not have noticed, how mortifying, how understandable.

Next, I ask the table, "What has been a turning point in your life?" and Sophie, also a woman in her thirties-ish who is sitting a few seats away from Katy, shares that she is currently figuring out what's next and how to dream again after her spouse died earlier this year. Katy and I immediately catch each other's eyes in a knowing glance.

After Sophie shares, people talk about leaving thirty-year marriages, changing majors in college, leaving their home countries for somewhere new, and starting over in so many ways. When we get all the way around, Katy says, "Well, I've been dancing around the specifics of my difficult season, but because you shared, Sophie, I want to say that I also lost my husband this year, just to say I know how vulnerable that is to share in a room full of strangers, to be the young person whose partner died, and how disorienting all of it is."

Here's what I love about this: Katy first takes care of herself by only sharing what feels comfortable to share, exploring what it felt like to *not* be the person who just lost her husband for the first time in forever. Then when she does share, it's an offering of solidarity to Sophie, letting her know that someone at the table knows acutely what she's going through. In a complete shift in posture from feeling like she has to "out" herself as The Grieving Widow, she's able to let Sophie know she is not alone.

Sophie, same as Katy, doesn't have to share about the loss of her partner, and it would have been completely appropriate for her to give herself the same permission Katy starts out with at the beginning of the night. But instead, because she does share, both she and Katy are able to discover that they are in similar stages, and we are able to witness them finding each other, as well as be moved by their stories.

With any act of vulnerability, no matter how minor (is there even such a thing as minor vulnerability?), we are opening ourselves up to be seen as we are, and therefore opening ourselves up to be possibly rejected, shut down, or misunderstood. It's vulnerable to ask *how are you?* earnestly, and it is vulnerable to answer with honesty. We hesitate to hold out the delicate, the fragile, the messy, because what if someone mishandles it, drops it, discards it, points out its faults and flaws? And yet every act of vulnerability makes it possible to be seen—and therefore known, understood, and even celebrated—for who we are, *as* we are. Vulnerability makes it possible for people to meet us where we're at.

What we get when we open ourselves up to the world is a world that rises to meet us. When we are soft, people soften. When we slow down and make space, people slow down, hunker in, and respond with a story. When we approach a conversation willing to have our minds changed, our worlds expand, our minds expand, our hearts expand. We find out that our neighbors lived in France for two years and the cashier loves the same band we do. We find out we're not the only ones who are struggling with nap time and potty training or job applications or phone addiction or loneliness. We find out a life hack for keeping our finicky plants alive. We get a new book suggestion. We find out we're not so alone in our wandering. We find a window into each other's worlds, which feel so separate and far away, but only as far away as the questions we're willing to ask each other while making sure that the person we're asking knows we really mean it: How are you? How are you today? How are you really?

When someone is the first to open the door of their lives to us, we can receive it as an invitation to meet each other. Some might call this an introduction, a progression, a result of exchanging information with one another. Some might call it communion.

5

Insufficiently Meeting Each Other

Ask for What We Need—and
Show Up How We're Able

Confession: I'm a long-standing curmudgeon about celebrating Valentine's Day. I *want* to love it—all the cute pink hearts and ruffled doilies and people walking the streets all day with massive bouquets of flowers for their partner or their mom. I am a deep believer in sharing with frequency and specificity what we appreciate about those we love. Ritualizing this practice with a holiday that seems widely commercial, however, leaves me wanting.

It's February 2024, and for the month's Dinner With Strangers theme, I am hoping to avoid being fully on the nose by talking exclusively about romantic relationships. Instead, I go with "How Do We Connect with Each Other?" and prepare dinner questions that touch on relationships and connection in general, trying to make our theme and conversation a little more expansive.

We start out by talking about what everyone's friendship superpowers are. I invite guests to finish the sentence "I'm the friend who…"—there are planners and breakers-of-plans, really good listeners and pep-talkers, someone who always sends a "have a great flight" text when their friends are traveling (which also means they remember when people's flights are—as someone who can barely remember my own travel itineraries, I was majorly impressed by this level of attentiveness) and itinerary organizers. There is a jokester in the group and a self-proclaimed troublemaker and the token you-should-break-up-with-your-boyfriender (okay, that was my answer—I'm the friend you call when it's time to plan the breakup conversation, and I'll give you my well-practiced speech and pour the wine).

Partway through the dinner conversation, I ask the group, "What is one way that someone could show up for you right now?" and people share that they want quality time and presence with their loved ones, they want to feel listened to and understood, they want reciprocity and communication in their partnerships, and they want to hear "I'm proud of you" and "You're doing okay" and "I see your effort." Someone shares that, as an overwhelmed mom, they would love for someone to come clean their fridge, and for someone, anyone, to tell them they're doing a good job. Someone wants grace when they need to withdraw and take time. Someone wants to find safe people and to be the person who shows up for themselves as much as they show up for others. Someone shares that they want people to meet them in their softness. Someone says that they want a divine intervention and wonders how much divinity is already around them if they were to stop and look for it.

Sid, a man in his early forties with kind eyes who's wearing an impressively crisp collared dress shirt, shares that he's been trying to get his best friend to connect more often, and on a deeper level. He says, "It feels like I'm always chasing him, always digging for connection, so finally a few weeks ago I told him I'd had enough. I said, 'Forget it. All I want is for you to just send me a selfie in the morning while you're having your coffee and show me what color of tie you chose for the day.' It's not enough, like I wish he would actually tell me how he's doing each day, but it felt like something attainable, and a way for us to say, 'Hi, this is me today, where are you?' And I didn't think he'd keep up with it, but it's been three weeks and we've sent a picture every day."

Everyone seems to lean into Sid as he's speaking. There is something particularly endearing about picturing this tall, seemingly buttoned-up, definitely professional, put-together man insisting that his (presumably) also professional, grown adult man best friend send him a picture every day with his morning coffee and daily tie of choice.

Sid's story strikes me as this incredible revelation of the reality of close relationships: Each of us has a need for human connection, and specific ways that make us feel seen, known, valued, prioritized, and appreciated. And because we each have our own specific ways that we prefer to connect, our people might often get it wrong, might not meet us in the way that we'd like to be met. Sid's friend, whether due to different wiring or priorities, or just due to the fact that carving out significant time to connect on a regular basis is a tall order in his busy life, couldn't "meet" Sid the way he ideally wanted to connect. And here's the beautiful thing: Sid came up with an alternative that may, on the surface, seem shallow or insufficient. But by doing so, Sid and his friend were connecting on the daily with their selfies and a quick check-in, creating a tiny window of connection through inviting each other into a small, literal snapshot of their day-to-day. Inevitably, along with the selfie, they'd send a snippet of an update: "The baby didn't sleep well at all last night" or "Big presentation today!" or "My in-laws are visiting this weekend!" By "giving up" his initial desire to connect in a "meaningful" way and instead suggesting this seemingly silly morning ritual, Sid actually found what he was looking for.

We have multiple people we are in a relationship with, and we have our busy lives and responsibilities and distractions that keep us from keeping each other in the loop, let alone connecting in a real, human, vulnerable present way. In this season of my life, for instance, I'm finding it really hard to keep in consistent contact within my friendships, especially with anyone who's not naturally in my daily or weekly orbit. I hardly have the words for "Everything is wild and strange and I'm grateful and tired and bewildered and excited and nervous and I feel like there are two dancing shrimp controlling my brain right now and everything is happening and nothing is official and I don't know when I can see you and don't know when we can talk and don't know what's going to happen but I love you and miss you and please don't give up on me."

In a perfect world, I'd have time for the voice notes and updates and check-ins and memes and FaceTimes; I barely have time to remind myself to stop and ask myself how *I'm* doing. And because of the insufficiency of quality time that I have to offer, I end up hermitting completely, not even attempting to reach out. But I *could* send a picture of me in-the-moment, wearing the same sweatshirt as yesterday. I could send a message like, "The big news of the day is that it's a hair wash day. Here I am in *this* day as it finds me, hammering through a to-do list that makes me want to cry a little bit. Hi."

———

A year after Sid tells his selfie story, my friend Rachel's wife dies unexpectedly. Rachel is, it goes without saying, reeling in grief. Rachel and I met at a retreat years ago, hitting it off immediately and becoming fast, kindred friends in the way you can in a retreat setting before returning to our separate lives on opposite sides of the continent—she in Redding, California, and me in Toronto. The cadence of our relationship is that we're infrequently in contact, but when we catch up over a call or a text blitz that usually starts with "Hey friend, what is going on in your world?" we seamlessly drop right into the deep.

When I see the news that her wife is gone, I send her a message right away. We send a few voice notes back and forth. Every word I can think of saying feels hollow; what is there to say other than *I am here, I see you, I'm so sorry*. I send a card and a book with my favorite page dog-eared, my favorite paragraph underlined. I wonder how to care for and support my friend from so far away.

A month passes, and I get a text from Rachel about a poem I shared online that mentions white sage from my friend's garden in Redding. "Is that me?!?! Is that *my* garden? *My* white sage? I love that!" her text says. We catch up a bit, blue text bubbles floating across our screens. I text, "How are you? Like, how are you *today* I guess." She responds, "Yeah, everyone keeps asking me that, and it feels like they're really asking, 'Are you better yet?' And like, um, my wife died. No, I'm not *better*. People ask because they care, but it is so hard to access how I am or update them or convey all the sadness. Where do I even begin?"

I recognize myself in the universal friend she's talking about: I want her to know I'm thinking of her, I want to check in, I want to be available to listen to how hard it's been, I want to bear witness to her pain. I don't want to give her work to do. I don't want her to feel like she has to *get into it*. I just want to be there for her, which is hard to do from so far away.

As Rachel and I are texting, Sid's selfie story comes to mind. I send Rachel a voice note, telling her the story—these two businessmen sending each other pictures of their coffees and their ties. "If you want…I know this is silly, but…we could do that. A way to check in and say hi and say *this is me today*. What do you think?" She responds with a picture, her funky glasses framing her placid blue eyes, slightly puffy from her passive tears, and a sad, hopeful smile peeking through her lips.

Over the next few months, we hardly miss a day. We send funny pictures, humbling pictures, pictures I'd never post to the internet, usually tomato-faced on my way back from the gym to make her laugh. "I guess I'm never getting cast in a Nike commercial with this blotchy face!" I say. I hold up coffee mugs close to the screen and text, "Maybe *this* is the coffee that will fix me!" Rachel sends a picture from on top of a ladder ("I tackled the gutters today! Taking care of things"), sends a picture from the garage ("I had to go through her things today"), sends a picture from a walk ("It feels good to get outside"), sends a picture after a heavy sob ("I can't believe she's gone forever"). Sometimes we talk about her wife, sometimes it's a quick check-in. I send her pictures from my desk, send her book progress updates ("Wrote one thousand words today, still scared the book is horrible!"). The daily ritual gives us the opportunity to share about how we're really doing or to offer something funny or to admit our fear, to address our pain. Sid's ritual became ours, and by lowering the barrier of entry to connection, we were able to meet each other daily, frequently, easily, with freedom and flexibility and without expectation of outcome.

We don't need a holiday, Valentine's Day or otherwise, to determine when and how we express our love. And also maybe it feels good to lean into the hokeyness of it. Or maybe you hate it and reject its consumerist attempt to get us to spend more, more, more. We don't need rules for how to check in with each other, and sometimes we need a friend like Sid insisting that we check in with a morning selfie, a proof-of-life text, a snippet from our day that reveals not much else other than the color of shirt we've chosen that day, maybe an accompanying text that may or may not let the other person know how we're feeling or what we're dreading or looking forward to in the day that lies ahead.

Ideally, we'd be regularly dialed into displays and gestures of affection and appreciation for each other, including but not limited to our romantic relationships. But you know what? Sometimes we get caught up in life. And sometimes the feelings are so big we don't even know where to start. And so some structure and guidance and an annual holiday to make sure we take a second to show our appreciation and express our feelings to each other aren't the worst thing.

Maybe celebrating Valentine's Day is like sending our morning selfie to each other: It barely scratches the surface. It doesn't give the full picture or provide in-depth, detailed information about what's going on or how we actually are. But when I send my best friend Catherine a purposefully ugly selfie showing my cheek zit that won't *kindly screw off*, what I mean is *hi, I love you and appreciate that you take me as I am*, and when I send my mom a text from the airport that says "kid on a leash," what I mean is *what a gift that I know all the ways to make you laugh*, and last year when I make this little card out of construction paper that says "Happy

Very Normal Wednesday!" on actual Valentine's Day and bring it with me to someone's house who isn't my boyfriend but there was *something* developing so we just ignored the fact that he's making me dinner on this national (commercial) holiday celebrating love, what I mean is *I think I like where this is going…and also I wish I knew what you were thinking,* and when I send eighteen emojis instead of a sentence in response to my friend Matt's all-caps text that says "HOW THE HELL ARE YOU," what I mean is *please accept these emojis as accurate modern hieroglyphics to my internal world and please take my silence to mean that I am overwhelmed with how long it's been since I've reached out.*

What I mean is, let's not hesitate to insufficiently, constantly reach for each other. What I mean is that there is so much to say, too much to say, and so much that is unsayable. And we should try with all our might anyway to say it with words and say it with actions and say it in whatever way we know how.

6

Are We Ever Asking What We Really Mean?

There's Usually a Question Under the Question

I am hanging out with Nicole and Audrey on Zoom after facilitating the workshop they've enrolled in for the month. At the beginning of 2022, to my bewilderment, I started facilitating online creative writing workshops: weekly two-hour sessions on Zoom for a month, with forums for prompts and sharing and peer critique throughout the week.

Diplomatic in my facilitatorship, I would *never* say that I have favorites within any cohort, workshop or dinner or otherwise. No, no, of course not. But I feel a kinship with these two right away—Audrey's funny, quippy retorts even in her first introduction to the group and her generous smile that lights up her whole face endear her to me right away. I love Nicole's evident softness, her slow, calm way of sharing, her reflective responses when people share their writing.

Nicole looks a bit bashful on her screen, nervously tapping her elbow, and asks, "Jess, I've been wondering, what do your days look like? What is your writing routine? What do you do day to day?" Taking her question at face value, I start rambling about my coffee addiction that occupies my first thoughts of every day and my fraught relationship with journaling, my ten-minute hip mobility routine that I follow on YouTube, my preference to do any creative writing in the morning and leave any administrative tasks or "business" writing for the afternoon.

After I've drabbled on for a while, Audrey asks her, "Did you ask Jess this because you're curious about her routine, or was there something more to your question? Are you looking for ways to switch up your own creative routine?" Nicole laughs a bit and sheepishly says, "Well, yeah, I just…so deeply want to be a full-time artist, and it just seems so far away for me, the leap seems too great. And I'm just wondering how anyone decides when they're ready to jump."

I feel quite embarrassed that I didn't think to ask this follow-up question, and I was so incredibly grateful for Audrey's inquiry. "Whoa!" I say. "Well, *this* is a *completely* different conversation!! Here I am going on about coffee intake when you're asking about cultivating a creative life and risk and leaping and going after what you want and how to be an artist in this weird world we live in. OKAY. Here we go."

Audrey's question back to Nicole has revolutionized the way I have conversations—I realize how bold that statement is. There is usually a *question under a question*; we present an initial question, maybe about a topic or about the person we're specifically speaking to, but of course there is the *Why* behind our question. Why are we curious about that? Why is it important to us? Why did this thing spark our interest? The *Why* might simply be a coincidence or something we have in common (someone says something about fishing and we are the world's biggest fishing enthusiast; someone mentions Barcelona and we are planning a trip there next year; someone has recently taken up veganism and, as we have taken the Pledge of the Vegans of the Universe, we too must announce that we are, in fact, a vegan as well). But even a commonality is, at its root, a place of connection, entwined in the soil of the unseen, and so someone asking more about our interests and travels and life-style is a way of saying *I think I found this starting point from which we can embark together.*

Likewise, there's a *Why* behind everything we sign up for, opt in to, and show up at: We're at the concert because it's our favorite band, or because the cute Swiss surfer we met in Ecuador said this song sounds like what it feels like to sit next to us on the beach at golden hour, or because this was the album we played on repeat after we got our heart broken that one time. We sign up for this gym because we saw a thing about taking care of our heart health (or because their intro offer was too good to miss, *two weeks unlimited for forty bucks,* are you kidding me?). We sign up for beginner ballet at thirty-six because we always wanted to dance but were too afraid of taking up space with our bodies. We go to this prayer group because we want to direct our worry or our hope in a particular direction. We don't step foot in a church anymore because of the reason we don't step foot in a church anymore. We show up because we have a reason. We say yes because we're looking for something.

We choose the things we choose because they resonate with something within us that feels alive. This means that, at any time, wherever we are, we have something real and true and important to inquire about each other that can bring us closer and help us understand each other better.

It has bewildered and humbled me every time I ask anyone at Dinner With Strangers what made them sign up. I started this project because I love hearing people's stories and wanted to create a place to listen to each other for the night, but the concept has resonated with people in so many more ways than I originally intended. People are coming because they're actively looking for deeper connection or they moved to the city four days ago and figured this would be the best place to inaugurate themselves into the neighborhood or because they just finalized their divorce or because their best friend just moved away or because they haven't felt like themselves in a while or because they wear too many false hats and want to take them all off or they want to see what it feels like to be anonymous without any of the titles they've been clinging to so tightly.

So now I make a practice at each dinner of asking people what brings them here: John says he's turning forty in ten days and this was a gift to himself to cap the last decade and to start the next one with intention and inspiration. Ellen says she has been at the lowest of the low after a relationship made her feel like she was nothing, and coming here was the first thing she's done for herself, a night to be inspired by a table of strangers who have made bold, brave choices. Akim says he hasn't been anywhere where he isn't in control of how people view him, and he wants to challenge himself to step out of the driver's seat of shaping people's perceptions. Kelly says she hasn't even eaten lunch alone in her whole adult life, and so why not do some exposure therapy and go have dinner with twenty strangers.

We often don't lead with our question under the question because we are fragile, tender creatures and it is delicate work to put our truest, most vulnerable selves out in the stark light of day. It's difficult to ask *can you tell me how you went about pursuing your dream because I too have a dream?* and so instead we ask about each other's morning routine. It's difficult to ask *do you have any clue how to navigate the world as it is now?* and so instead we ask about each other's morning commute. It's difficult to ask *did this come easily to you? Because I am having difficulty with even the very first step,* and so instead we ask about weekend plans. It's difficult to admit we want something deeply or have a deep ache or a deep fear or that we feel incredibly, deeply lost and confused and we're probably the only person who feels this way, has ever felt this way, so we'd better not find out if that's in fact true because then on top of being the only person who is lost and confused, now everyone also knows how lost and confused we are.

It is no small thing to put our truest questions out there—to the world at large, or to each other. Every question is an outstretched hand, with the possibility that our hand might be swatted away or that it will stay empty. What a relief whenever someone immediately places something in our palm, their answer and insight like placing a precious pebble in our fist, or better yet, taking our hand in theirs and walking us home.

We can unlock a whole new way of connecting when we slow down enough to listen for the question under the question or are bold enough to ask what we really mean until we find all the *Whys* hidden just below the surface.

7

We Have So Much Time / We Have So Little Time / We Have No Idea How Much Time We Have at All

Dreams Are Patient

Gloria arrives at dinner with a softness that is palpable. Her style is unfussy and graceful; she is dressed in drapey, soft, all-black clothing, her peppered silver hair pulled back in a low bun. The way she is holding her purse in front of her as a buffer gives a slight nod to the fact that she is perhaps a bit nervous and tentative, the bag acting like soft leather armor as she enters the room. (I had a therapist who once made a comment about the way most of her clients—myself included—subconsciously reach for one of the throw pillows on the couch during their sessions, some drawing it close as a safeguard, others clinging for dear life, holding it in their lap like a superhero's shield, as if the floral pattern might buffer the edges of whatever's being shared. I would twirl the soft tassels lining the edge between my fingers as I practiced saying difficult things out loud.)

When she speaks, Gloria takes her time with her words, each one feeling like it is said on purpose. The way she sits has a calmness about it: ankles crossed neatly, her hands woven together gently in her lap, no fidgeting or excessive movement. She speaks with a soft timbre and a quiet voice, but it shouldn't be mistaken for meekness. She has the kind of voice that you'd want reading you a bedtime story, a poem, a prayer. At one point during dinner, I interrupt her to ask if she can speak up a bit, because every word I catch feels like gold, and some of what she's saying is difficult to hear at our sprawling table of twenty people.

I ask the group to share something new they're introducing into their life, and Gloria shares, "I've been learning to ask myself, 'What do you want?' and that's a very new thing for me. I am the youngest child in my family, and all my siblings told me what to do and what I should like and where I should go my whole life. My clothes were hand-me-downs; I wore what they had worn. I took the classes they took. I am fifty-eight, and I started therapy for the first time this year, and my therapist has been helping me with this—trying to tap into my desire, or even a preference, for goodness' sake! The other day she asked me, 'What did you dream about when you were a little girl?' and that unlocked something in me. A dream I was too timid to ever admit or go after. And now, this year, I'm finally making moves to go after it." Gloria doesn't elaborate on what her dream is, and the way she shares it with us made me feel like it's too tender, too precious, to ask her in front of everyone.

As we get up from the dinner table and move on to mingling around the room with dessert, I make my way over to Gloria to ask her what she's dreaming about, if she's willing to share. "Oh! My dream?!" She blushes but clearly lights up from the inside. She covers her mouth slightly and lifts her shoulders to shelter herself in, like she's about to whisper a secret. "When I was little, I wanted to be an actress. Which of course everyone thought was silly—how could that be a real profession? So I never did anything about it. And at the beginning of this year, I thought, *What am I waiting for?* I started taking voice lessons; I found a voice acting coach. And you know what? I've booked some things! Actual commercials on TV and some radio slots! Can you believe it?!" she says with a giggle. I stand with my mouth agape. "How wild," I say, "that the dream was there quietly all along and has now shown up in a way you couldn't have imagined or planned." Here she was, at fifty-eight, finally pursuing what she'd always thought about doing. Here she was, trying for trying's sake, because she wanted to.

We talk for a while about the timing of things: How we can't write our own story better than the weird universe can, despite our best efforts. How we might think we gave something up a long time ago, only to see it return to us years and years later. We note the patience of dreams: They wait for us while we make up decades of excuses, let other priorities take precedence, let other people's opinions guide our choices. We sometimes tuck our dreams away in a proverbial shoe box in the closet, telling ourselves we can take it down from the shelf anytime and then forgetting after a while that we put it away in there. We go on to do many other reasonable, practical, impressive, reliable things. Other dreams may arrive and eclipse previous ones. And still the dream may find new ways to try to get our attention. Three small dreams stacked on each other's shoulders in a trench coat, ringing the doorbell: Don't think they won't try it. Dreams get crafty, they meld and melt, they take new forms, they rattle and they wait.

Gloria's pursuit of her girlhood dream brings to mind my nineteen-year-old self, confused and tired and feeling like a failure after not *making it* as a musician within one year of moving to the big city. I was comparing the pacing of my dream to how those around me were finding success and making a name for themselves. I was unable to see that each of our roads was our own to walk.

It brings to mind so many instances when friends and strangers alike decide against pursuing a dream because it seems preposterous to start from scratch, or start over, or take a hard pivot to a different kind of life *at their age*: Heather giving up acting because she hadn't made it big at twenty-five. Courtney staying with her cheating boyfriend because she couldn't imagine finding her own apartment and going on dating apps at thirty-eight. Steven, at fifty-four, telling me that he hasn't done something outside of his routine in seventeen years.

I think about how many times I've told myself or heard others declare that it's too late or we missed the thing or how could any of our circumstances change, when the reality is there could very well be a version of our lives that we've dreamed about that just hasn't arrived to us yet.

———

I move to Toronto at nineteen with about $600 in my bank account after paying first and last month's rent. That $600 feels like a lot of money to me (it's a lot of hours when your wage is $8.90/hour) until I realize I don't have any furniture and I have to start buying everything for myself—not just coffees and movie tickets but paper towels, dish soap, eggs (which is to say: sustenance)—every day. I'm here with a dream in my heart and a vision of how the timing of that dream is going to come to fruition but no understanding of or experience with what it means to implement a plan.

The dream: Become a famous melancholy folk musician.

The timing: Um, that should take approximately a few months, right?

The plan: Well, I've written all these songs and already have my setlist ready to go. My friends Matt and Tom booked us a show in the back room of Duffy's Tavern, so we're already hitting the ground running, and people will hear about me after that, and then *it* will…*happen.*

What happens is that I have to find a job (or three) to pay my $480/month rent. I hand out a slew of résumés at coffee shops, restaurants, and clothing stores for twenty blocks along Queen Street one afternoon before a kind restaurant manager points out that my résumé doesn't have a single shred of contact information, just my name in a too-large bold font, centered at the top. After that, I call it a day and take myself out for a sandwich at a restaurant where I hadn't dropped a résumé off.

I play shows in loud bars in front of my three roommates (bless them for showing up to each one) and six to twelve other people over and over again. I find it hard to play my guitar and write songs in our apartment with paper-thin walls after working a double: one shift at the coffee shop in the morning, followed by one banquet bartending shift at the hotel at night. And then, after ten months of not really writing a song and not recording an album and not having an agent or anything fancy or business-y or official on the go, I think I've failed. I think I've squandered the dream. I think I was wrong about what I thought I loved and what I thought I was maybe-good-at or could-be-good-at if I tried a bit harder with a bit of help. I think I've missed the boat.

———

Years later, I'm visiting my family on the West Coast, and I drive down to Washington state to visit my Aunt Mona (my dad's sister, for those keeping track of the family cameos). We are hardly ever on the same coast at the same time, let alone continent; Mona has lived in Switzerland and Singapore, Ethiopia and New Mexico. We revel in the time we get to spend together in the same room.

Mona and I launch right into the middle of the (metaphorical) lake while staring out at the literal one her cabin overlooks, hints of spring starting to flirt with the trees that climb the mountain ridge. She tells me about the new coaching program she's enrolled in, starting in June, that will allow her to start her own company after decades of volunteer and pro bono work abroad because of my uncle's role in his own career, because *workplace politics* etc., because *motherhood*, maybe, partially, because priorities, because, because. My aunt prioritized time with her kids during their teenage summers instead of signing up for a master's program or writing PhD papers. Sitting at her kitchen table, we marvel at how life was good and gracious in the way that there has been time enough for both: to be present during those foundational years for my cousins and to pursue a career of her own now that they've flown the cozy nest she built around them. She thought at the time that she was making a choice between one life and another, when really it was a choice of which sequence her goals and priorities were going to take.

So much of life comes in seasons: There's the season of young dreams and cramped apartments and, for many of us, crappy jobs that demand a lot and pay very little. There are seasons of clarity, of monotony, of doubt, of repetition. If you go on to have kids, there's the season of parenting tiny humans, getting no sleep, not knowing which way is up, trying to keep everyone alive and everyone fed and everyone from throwing [insert all the things babies throw] across the room. The season of playing soccer and hanging out with friends and wanting to play ukulele or take tap dancing lessons or be on the debate team. The season of *who even am I anymore?* and *do I have an identity outside this hamster wheel of a life we're living?* The season of *who even is my spouse?* and *do we even like each other anymore?* The season of *what next?* The season of *everyone has moved out oh wait no they haven't oh yes they're gone oh wait.* The season of *how are we old enough to have kids who are getting married?* The season of *what do I want and when was the last time I asked myself that question?* None of it lasts forever and some seasons are simultaneous and overlapping, just as our identities and the titles and names we call ourselves are simultaneous and over-lapping. We look around and say *I guess this is who I am now; I guess this is my life.* We forget that we have been many things and will continue to grow and change many times over before the end of the story.

On a recent flight, I sit next to a thirty-four-year-old ER doctor and we talk for four hours. We share about pursuing our dreams and how beautiful/difficult/hard/unlikely that is, and what we're learning in therapy (what, you don't talk to strangers beside you on a plane about what you're learning in therapy?) and diagnosing our ADHD via TikToks we've seen and what we're learning / thinking / not learning about love.

She tells me her partner is lovely and kind and so, so boring, like nothing-in-common boring, like how-can-you-possibly-feel-fulfilled-in-your-life boring, like most-likely-unsatisfied-in-his-life-but-won't-admit-it boring. (Who knows if the gentleman in question is actually boring, but *she* is definitely bored.) She says she will be with him forever because of *reasons,* because mostly he has been so great, so she "can't" leave. Because she's thirty-four, like the number itself is some sort of explanation. And I think to myself, *She should leave*—this person I know really nothing about except that her therapist's name is Carmen and she, like me, treats herself to an overpriced airport treat from the overpriced airport kiosk (preferably kettle corn in her case, which she is currently sharing with me across the empty middle seat between us). I wonder how we get to the place where we feel so irreversibly down a specific road because of the time investment we've put into something.

I guess I should rephrase this to say that I would (probably) leave if I were her. I would hope that I would leave because not being able to bring yourself to go is not a reason to stay.

I think about how long life is when you are with the "wrong" person, when you stay with them because you are afraid that the imaginary "right" (air quotes applied generously in both cases) person might not exist out there—you don't know for sure—and so you stay.

It's December 2023, and I'm at my friend Kim's funeral. She was thirty-six, and I know everyone says that someone they know has the best laugh, but everyone is wrong actually because Kim's laugh is, in fact, the best laugh that's ever existed. She died right before Christmas from breast cancer. A mother to two impossibly adorable little girls. An incredibly talented elementary school teacher, the kind you dream of for your kids. A wife, married to the love of her life. She and Scotty were one of those couples who you know have that Extra-Magical Thing, the no-doubt-in-my-mind-they're-soulmates thing. Best friends. Laughed hysterically together all the time. Got a kick out of each other. Spoke so highly of each other at all times in all rooms to all people. Teased the shit out of each other. They're the couple who would be on the postcard of the ninety-year-olds holding hands on the beach wearing goofy visors, her boobs tucked into her golf shorts, his earlobes down to the ground, etc., etc., except they're not ninety and she never will be, which is absolutely horrible and impossibly stupid and unfathomable.

After his speech, Scotty plays a video he's compiled of Kim laughing, of her dancing, her chatting with their daughters; videos he'd taken of her just muddling around their house, late-night chicken wings in the kitchen when they were new parents, and a clip of their first dance at their wedding. And then a clip of them dancing in the hospital to the same song, ventilator strung on her radiant face, Scotty's cheeks soaked in tears. I stand there overcome with the brutal unfairness of it. And the brutality that fairness has nothing to do with it. There is no barter or deal that any of us could have made to get her more time, to heal her body, to get her to ninety or sixty-five or forty on that beach with Scotty. There is only the time we all had with her, which will never be enough.

I imagine all these women sitting at a table together: Gloria signing up for her first vocal coaching session at fifty-eight; my Aunt Mona wondering if she was trading one life for another and then realizing there is time enough for all of it; the ER doctor on the plane worrying it's too late to start over in anything, being afraid of what it would mean to have wasted her time, and so staying where she is; Kim with way too little time, no time left at all. And I'm there somewhere with them, thumbing the metaphorical clock in my hands, wondering about its battery life.

We are each given this life with its mysteriously numbered days. All I can say is I'm glad that in this lifetime I've made it to this table, with these friends, and here at this table, miraculously, with all of you.

I don't know if we'll make it to all the versions of ourselves we want to be. I like this version of us, with these questions, here, just fine. There is time enough. We haven't got long.

The Universality of Our Singular Stories

There Are Ties Between Each of Our Experiences

One thing that happens after someone violates your body is that it pummels a crater into the core of your being, shelled out like an echoing canyon where something soft and living used to be. There is no getting back to normal; that shit turns you into something else.

Another thing that happens is that you start to understand the universality of everything: that my own singular and specific experience is tied to every injustice that's ever happened. Every hand that has grazed any thigh like it's being conquered and any gaze that has objectified any body and anything that's ever been taken without consent since the beginning of time belongs to all of us, was done to all of us, is all of ours to carry and call out. This, specifically, is the universality of grief: We don't have to lose the exact same thing in the same way in order to recognize that it's all the same ache with a slightly different name. Maybe the world is gracious in some backward way: that nothing ugly and unimaginable has to be faced alone.

I'm the type of privileged that, previous to the assault, allowed me to naively think that the powers that be are in place and equipped to protect us. I could cognitively make sense of a creepy guy doing a creepy thing. What I couldn't make sense of was a crown lawyer[1] who couldn't have been more than five years older than me sitting me down in a tiny room of the courthouse, telling me she was throwing my case out. There wasn't enough evidence to bring it to a trial, not even with the people who saw me run out of the room sobbing and saw him chasing after me while yelling, "Jess, please don't say anything," and heard me ask for help and his pathetic confession in front of all of them and his boss saying she always knew he was vile in an attempt to let me know she believed me. I sat in that room with the crown lawyer and felt like I was having that dream where I'm screaming at the top of my lungs in a room full of people and no one will turn around to help me. I stared straight into that lawyer's eyes and asked her, "What kind of hope can we even believe in if *this* kind of case doesn't even make it to a courtroom?" and also, "How do you live with yourself?"

She didn't respond to either question.

I understand *what it has to do with me* with every story that

---

1 The Canadian equivalent to a state prosecutor.

comes after mine: My friend was held down at a party when she was fifteen and those boys are now men with wives and girlfriends and children and they probably don't even remember and she has to think about them every day. We all sit around in a karaoke bar on a Tuesday, and one by one, everyone ends up telling a story kind of like this or not like this but the same anyway. Fifty-eight women have to offer up their story before a famous comedian even sees the inside of a courtroom and a music mogul continues assaulting women for years without consequence and in fact is protected by his other famous friends. A guy in high school assaults a fellow student and goes on to be appointed to the Supreme Court. A morally bankrupt creep becomes the president of an entire country not just once but then a second time, his rap sheet of crimes made inconsequential by seventy million people saying he's the guy for the job.

So when I say that nobody is coming to save us, I mean that the system is supposed to take care of a whole lot and doesn't; not accountability, not school lunch programs, not keeping kids safe, not gun reform, not bodily autonomy, not access to health care. It does not believe women, stop billions of dollars of bombs from dropping on the heads of children, or look after anyone vulnerable. Justice is slow and fairness is a fantasy and we live in a land that is ruled by money and power and greed. The structures that we have in place are insufficient and fail us every day.

When I say that we are all we have, I'm talking about the fact that what saved me had nothing to do with The Powers That Be and everything to do with the miraculous, simple care from the people surrounding me: Natasha leaving work without me even asking her to and lying on the floor with me right after it happened. The dried lavender that Erin brought home and put on the table to offer me something healing. Ryan washing my hair so delicately the next day. Matt and Mel going to the initial hearing just to stand vigil if nothing else. My mom just existing in my world. Rashid trying his hardest to love me during that impossible year. The man who waited behind me at the subway station as I held up the line saying he had all the time in the world. Marilyn putting her soft hands over mine at the art gallery, saying she knows it's been a hard year, hasn't it, and sitting with me in the quiet impossibility of it all. Matthew lighting white sage from Rachel's garden in Redding early in the morning before the civil litigation hearing. None of them waited for anyone else to do the right thing. None of them thought that they could make it right. They simply didn't hesitate to do good when they saw the opportunity in front of them.

What I'm saying is that it feels like The System is only built to serve and protect everything corrupt and awful, and it feels like it's never going to change and that there is so much to fix and that nothing will move the needle or flip the tide and everyone is too preoccupied or lazy or apathetic or distracted or selfish to do anything for the greater good. What I'm saying is that it feels like the world is irrevocably fucked in many ways.

Sometimes the swiftness and depth of our empathy depend on how closely we relate to each other's experience. I recognize that there's something to that; my sister tells us that her friend's three-year-old has died in a car accident. The news makes my knees feel like goo, makes me physically wince, makes me want to bellow on this stranger's behalf, and I'm sure it is felt even more intensely by my sister, who knows this family personally, and she's the mother of her own two young kids. My sister relates to their story in a more personal way, but luckily empathy isn't some complex and delicate chemistry equation, needing a *specific* amount of relatability or the *right* amount of understanding someone's experience exactly in order to care for each other, otherwise the science project will be ruined.

We often hear people speak of assault survivors as someone's sister, someone's daughter, someone's mother, someone's wife. We hear men say over and over, "Now that I have daughters of my own, I see the world differently…" Relatability does make someone's story hit closer to home. But when we realize that all injustice is universal, regardless of the specifics, every daughter, mother, wife, son, neighbor, stranger becomes a human, a human who intrinsically deserves our support, a human who intrinsically deserves protection and advocacy and safety and love and grace and understanding. The quicker we are to relate to the universality of our stories, the quicker we are to care about, and for, each other.

In rebuttal to the pretty-much-hopelessness of the state of How Things Are, every single gesture of softness becomes a revolution: the meals we make for each other and the baby we smile at on the bus and every song we send with a text saying *hey, this made me think of you* and the trans flag that someone places in the corner of the window of the bakery to let our neighbors know they're safe here and the letters we write to our representatives even though we've been saying the same thing in every letter for over a year and every time we ask each other *can you help me understand what that was like for you?* and every poem we read out loud (or to ourselves in the quiet of our loneliness) and every time we ask ourselves what small, minuscule kind thing could I do for someone else, and then go do that thing. With each of these actions, we create a different world.

It all means nothing. It is the only thing that counts.

9

Queering the Table

Coming Out Is a Sacred Act

At most of the dinners I've cohosted with Ryan, he usually shares a version of his story about coming out to his family. Sometimes he mentions it in passing, explaining that his family is really supportive of him. Sometimes he mentions it as we're discussing identity, our understanding of ourselves, or societal expectations and pressure. Sometimes he talks about it in the context of the different expressions of masculinity within his family of farmers and athletic, "supermasculine" brothers. And sometimes he tells the story from start to finish: Growing up on the farm. Feeling *different* from his brothers and not having the language for why. Being a late bloomer. Having a circle of (girl) friends who kept him safe and loved him as he was, for who he was. Going off to college in a still-small-town-but-not-as-small-as-the-town-he-was-from, and discovering and exploring his sexuality for the first time. The letter he rewrote a million times before emailing it to his parents and brothers. Why he felt like emailing them was the best way: so they could experience their initial reaction as it came out of them without him having to witness it. His older brother sending a separate email to the others (excluding Ryan), telling them they all have one opportunity for their initial reaction to be one of support and love and acceptance, and they better not mess that one opportunity up.

Ideally, coming out feels like a liberating, expressive proclamation of someone's most elemental attributes. But because we live in a bigoted world, coming out is much more layered than that—even dangerous in many cases. It's not simply informing someone about identity markers; it's disclosing something that might be weaponized against us, making us the target of someone's judgment, harassment, and discrimination. This means that queer people often withhold fundamental parts of their identity when introducing themselves as a means of self-protection, and rightfully so. It puts on full display that it is a radical act to show up fully as ourselves in any room, how there is incredible privilege to get to do so, and invites us to consider how we can make the spaces we inhabit safer for everyone, that we all might feel emboldened and safe to introduce ourselves in our fullest, truest expressions.

Various queer friends occupy a spectrum of opinions on the necessity to come out in any official way. Matt tells me he never talked to his family about his sexual identity; he just told his parents that he'd started seeing someone and could Charlie please join them for family dinner on Thursday night? He questions, "Why do gay people have to declare their identity so blatantly and straight people don't?" Carly comes out to her best friend Grace, who tells their whole varsity volleyball team, taking away Grace's autonomy to introduce herself as she'd like, to whom she'd like, when she'd like. Tom, born into an Orthodox religion, first comes out as a confession—literally *in* confession—to his priest.

"But you don't have a limp wrist!" the priest says to a terrified, made-to-feel-shameful Tom. He replies, "Be that as it may, Father…" The priest tells him not to worry, they'll get him married off to a nice girl and he won't have to think about it again. Tom spends the next eighteen years celibate, suppressing his desire and self-expression, denying himself the right to love, not telling anybody about his sexuality—except God, whom he prays to every day, asking for this "broken" part of him to be cured. At thirty-eight, Tom finally concedes that, if God doesn't make mistakes, then maybe he isn't broken because of who he loves and how he feels after all.

As a straight, white, cisgender woman in a heteronormative society, I am not required (or invited) to go through the process of examining and then declaring who I am, what I'd like to be known as, and known for, and how the way I love shapes the way I move through the world. And because of these most basic ways I identify—in regard to my race, my gender expression, my sexual orientation—any version of sharing these markers mostly doesn't feel like I'm *disclosing* information. It doesn't immediately put me in harm's way with the bigots (though society has plenty of other ways to weaponize my sex and gender). When introducing myself or describing myself, I consider how deep I want to go without the added layer of evaluating whether I'm opening myself up for judgment or harassment. With this in mind, I see coming out in divergence from what we deem "normative" as radical in any context and completely understandable why many omit and withhold these parts of themselves.

There are so many things that form my understanding of self: the people I'm drawn to, what attraction means to me, what clothes I choose that make me feel most myself, my understanding and presentation of my gender, what communities and cultures I am a part of, and what traits, values, and beliefs I hold. If we were going to do an exploratory exercise to define each of these things, we'd quickly see that our personal definitions of each vary greatly.

It is a sacred act for any of us to examine, and then attempt to define, the names and titles that express our understanding of ourselves. Anyone who's willing to share how they know themselves to be should be received with incredible reverence.

There is no "normal" way to carve a path, live a life, choose a career, or define our values. There is only the life each of us has in front of us, and our own understanding of ourselves as the person walking it. How absurd to think I could know anything about someone's path before they've told me what it's like to be them?

It's 2018. I've started volunteering as a writing facilitator with the Writers Collective of Canada, a nonprofit that hosts writing workshops for vulnerable communities. I'm partnered with Anne, a retired elementary school teacher with a warm, calm presence that radiates like a soft light. We're leading a six-week writing workshop at a drop-in center in our neighborhood that offers daily meals, medical care, community resources, and social and developmental programming. We're encouraged to come early and eat lunch with participants before our 1 p.m. sessions, so Anne and I show up at noon to gather around the table for hot, heaping bowls of chili.

During our first workshop, we invite our participants to share their name and play Two Truths and a Lie—everyone shares three "facts" about themselves and the group must determine which one isn't true. Darrin shares that he was born in a car, has met the Pope, and is allergic to strawberries (after we guess, we find out he was, in fact, born at home—he arrived so quickly that his mother delivered him right in the middle of the living room. I don't recall where he ran into the pope…). Ethel shares that she's the youngest of eight kids, loves to paint, and her favorite band is the Rolling Stones (just kidding! Her favorite band is actually Depeche Mode!). When it's Anne's turn, she shares, "I'm a great cook, I love to garden, and I've known I was gay since I was eight years old." A few people's heads shoot up in curious attention when she shares her third fact—Darrin in particular looks quite shocked, unable to keep his jaw from dropping. Anne's facts are a departure from the more surface-level intros that people are sharing, and given the setting, it's incredibly vulnerable of her to come out right away. The group pauses for a second, and someone says, "I bet you're a terrible cook," and we all break out into laughter before carrying on with our workshop.

Afterward, as we're debriefing the workshop, Anne shares more about her intention behind sharing about her orientation: "I was a little nervous to start out with a bit of a bang, but it's really important to me that I share about my queerness after so many years of keeping it a secret. My partner and I have been together for over thirty years, and I was teaching all that time. I was only 'out' at the very last school I taught at before retiring. When I first started teaching, I very well might have lost my job if the school board knew I was gay and living with my partner. Certainly, it would've caused outrage with certain parents. Not being out was a matter of protection, a matter of survival, for my livelihood and my safety. But I'm done hiding."

Anne kept this part of her identity as a necessary secret in her professional life at what I can only imagine is a monumental personal and emotional expense. It makes me wonder about the effects of hiding parts of ourselves in the name of self-preservation and self-protection—withholding may be the safest thing to do, making it the best course of action, but it certainly carves away at our spirit. Anytime we feel misunderstood, unwelcome, or over-looked, the work is put on us to decide whether we are able to push back, attempt to clarify or correct, or "out" and "other" ourselves despite the potential consequences.

I'm eating breakfast at a yoga and writing retreat I'm cohosting, sitting next to Ali, who is queer and nonbinary; they work as a yoga teacher in Ottawa. I led the retreat-goers in our own version of Dinner With Strangers the night before to open the weekend, and over dinner Ali shared a story about an inspiring queer yoga night they'd recently attended. Now at breakfast, I ask if they can share a bit more about why the class was so transformative for them, and they share, "Well, it's always just such a relief to be in queer spaces because everyone is operating with the premise that *everyone* is different. There are no preconceived notions that we have anyone *figured out*, because how could we? We're strangers! Any expression of titles or identity or pronouns or experience is shared simply as a way of introducing ourselves—it's not explaining ourselves, outing ourselves, or othering ourselves."

Incredibly moved by Ali's experience, I start talking with them about what it would look like to queer the table at Dinner With Strangers, or any space where people are convening; at a gathering where we're asking people to share their unique experiences and singular accounts of who they are and how they show up in the world, there should be no assumption that any one person is similar to another or sees the world the same way we do. By defining ourselves individually, we see the threads of the universal while witnessing that there are so many ways to define a life. It brings to mind bell hooks's words on understanding queerness beyond sexual orientation. She explains, "'Queer' not as being about who you're having sex with (that can be a dimension of it); but 'queer' as being about the self that is at odds with everything around it and that has to invent and create and find a place to speak and to thrive and to live."[1] Specific to hooks's anti-oppression framework from which she taught us, the concept of queerness is not just about self-expression but about self-*creation*. And any time we gather, we create our own way of connecting, our own way of gathering, unique to the people in the room, the stories and histories we come with, and where we decide to go together.

I've started to ask myself in what ways do the events I host have a baseline of "normalcy" or "sameness"? How can I change that? Perhaps even by instating the rule that no one can say what they do for work, I'm removing our usual societal normativity of defining ourselves by our job titles and thus inviting everyone into introducing themselves in new ways—our own version of coming out to each other.

Taking ownership of the names and titles and identifying markers we claim for ourselves is a holy, sacred practice. One of the most common conversations I get to have with people in my creative community is whether or not they are "allowed" to claim the title

---

1   hooks, bell. 2014. "Are You Still a Slave? Liberating the Black Female Body." The New School, New York City.

Writer for themselves, as opposed to *a person who writes some things.* Sure, they write, sure, their chest burns with an unceasing fire when they read certain poems, sure, they stay up late at night pouring their soul onto paper and trying to find the perfect way to describe the feeling pulsing through their chest, but can they really call themselves a *Writer?*

When I insist that being a writer and, more generally, a creative, is a vocation (the way they move through the world) and not simply a job title (something that describes where you're employed and that you get paid for that work), I can feel their whole bodies relax, their spirits lighten.

When we find the words and names to express who we are, we give shape to the home that is ourselves, the fortress that makes us up that no one can claim for themselves, that no one can take away. No one can tell me what to do with this inner room, or what to make of the garden growing (or not growing, SOS) inside me. No one can tell me that I can't sleep with all the windows open, or which lights to keep on, how many candles is too many candles for one abode. No one can tell me what to call this place. That is for me to name.

I wonder what it would look like if we all continually came out to each other (only in spaces where it doesn't feel obligatory or as if it were some heavy confession to declare our true nature to those around us). What if we all started partaking in declaring and claiming who we know ourselves to be? What are we missing by thinking that the practice of examining the intricacies of the way we identify isn't for everybody? What paths have been forged by our queer beloveds who have, out of necessity, out of lifesaving proclamation, shown us the way?

Here is the gift within the gift of this practice: In order to declare who we are, we must first do the work of examining ourselves, our lives, and where we feel the most ourselves, what we adorn our bodies in to feel the most ourselves, and what embodied love looks like (love toward others *and* toward ourselves). If we are to declare who we are, we must first meet ourselves and discover what we know to be true. If we're being honest, that can be a terrifying practice, because for our first go at it, we might not come up with much. It takes our whole lifetime to meet ourselves. So we'd better get to it.

I want each of us to feel free to introduce ourselves in the truest, freest ways. I want us to feel safe, able, and encouraged to do the tender work of asking ourselves who we are and what names and titles and identifying words make us feel at home in ourselves. I want us to do this as many times as we need to, meeting ourselves over and over again, letting ourselves be surprised by what we find. And I want to live in a world where it is safe for all of us to do this in our fullest expressions.

And while we work on that safe world, I want us to fight ferociously for those of us who don't have the privilege of *simply existing* without having our identities and orientations and self-expressions questioned and attacked.

Let us uphold a world where we can all meet each other in the truest, softest, fullest ways.

10

Two Strangers Converge at a Table

Lean Into Our Differences

I've always had a funny ritual around placing each guest's name card around the table. It's kind of ridiculous, since every person is a stranger to me, no name differentiating anyone from anyone else.

I walk circles around the table, shuffling the name cards like a deck of cards.[1] I'm not all-in on *energy stuff*, not sure how *all of that* works exactly—and isn't that the whole point of the spirit, or whatever name you have for it, that guides us, that it remains something of a mystery? I'd at most like to marvel that there's *something* going on, and that I've set enough tables and been at the helm of enough rooms to know that I've got to get my whole being *in the zone* on event days—*channeling* whatever that kinetic mystery is. I

---

1 I was going to say like a blackjack dealer, but let's be serious now: It's more like a toddler who doesn't know which card to play on their turn in Go Fish.

picture some fun puppeteer pulling on the universe strings when deciding who ends up sitting next to each other at every Dinner With Strangers that I host.

Maybe it's funny to have "assigned" seating at a dinner where everyone is a stranger anyway; seating charts are for controlling and ensuring flow of conversation, keeping dueling relatives away from each other at family gatherings, balancing the introvert/extrovert ratio, putting the salesperson next to the one who's in the market for whatever they're selling, etc. At Dinner With Strangers, all I have to go on is that this person is named Peter and this person is named Cory.

If nothing else, I hope the name cards offer people a slight feeling of belonging and intention. It removes that feeling for the last person to sit down at the table that they're simply taking whatever spot is left. It mixes up the conversation and connections that form in the first forty-five minutes of the event before we get to the table.

I've always had a sense of ease around last-minute cancellations, or I should say: I feel like there's some magic at play when people take last-minute tickets after someone has to cancel. Ryan and I always had the mantra "Whoever's meant to be at the table will make it to the table," believing that the alchemy created at each dinner is specific to the exact combination of people who end up at each dinner, never to be re-created again. It always feels a little extra magical to have a guest list set one specific way, only to have a little shuffle or two in the last twenty-four hours leading up to the event when someone sees a ticket that becomes available last minute and says, "You know what, why not? Maybe it's meant to be."

———

Twenty-three guests are heading my way on a sticky August day. The theme for this specific Dinner With Strangers is "The Stories We Share." There's been a last-minute ticket situation—someone coming down with the flu yesterday—resulting in Sarah scooping up the available spot within minutes. I wake up to a message from her early in the morning saying that she can't find the email with the exact address for the event and she needs to know when to get on the road since she's driving from Pennsylvania to Toronto. I resend the info email, wish her safe travels, look up how far the drive from Pennsylvania to Toronto even is for my own knowledge, and get ready to head to the event space.

Cut to 6 p.m., and guests begin to arrive, the last of them being Sarah, a smidge late and in a bit of a fluster. She comes rushing in like a bright, warm light, as if someone pulled open the curtains right at golden hour. She has an infectious laugh and embraces me as if she's welcoming *me* to the evening ahead. Needless to say, I'm immediately drawn to her and excited to hear what she'll share throughout the night.

Eventually, I gather the group in a circle for our first round of conversation to introduce ourselves and break the ice. Inspired by our theme, I ask my first question: "What fictional character from a storybook or movie do you most relate to?" The entire room stares at me with wide, stressed-out owl eyes, drawing a blank, and, being the *professional* that I am, I pivot on the spot. (That's a bit of a humblebrag, forgive me.) I try again, asking, "If we were planning a heist together, what would your role be?" People jump on board with this silly hypothetical, getting really creative and specific with their answers: "I'd drive the getaway car but also be the one to mess up the heist because the music would be so loud that I'd miss the rest of you running toward me and not start it in time," "I'd be the one sitting y'all down one by one asking, *Okay, but do you actually want to do this?*" "I'd be the one who'd miss the heist because I forgot to put it in my Google Calendar."

Jane, an incredibly elegant woman with the most perfect chin-length bob I've ever seen, says, "Listen: I'd be in the control room with every single person's role planned out in a color-coded binder. I'd know the heist with variation A–Z, Z–A, forward and backward. I'm pulling levers and telling everyone where to go over the walkie-talkie. Nothing's going wrong on my watch." We collectively agree that Jane is officially in charge of our hypothetical heist, no question.

Sarah, standing next to Jane, marvels at Jane's evident organization and thoroughness. She exclaims, "Oh my! I need Jane to take over everything! I've never had an organized day in my entire life. I do everything last minute—bought a ticket to this dinner yesterday, drove up this morning, I don't even know where I'm staying tonight!" Jane's eyes go wide as Sarah continues, "I once moved my family three states over with thirty days' notice without looking at the house we moved into because my friend told me we'd like it there. I could be in charge of a lot, but just don't count on me to actually show up because I'll probably forget that I said yes!!"

"But what if you can't find a hotel?!" Jane asks, clearly shocked. Sarah responds matter-of-factly, "It's a big city, as if there won't be a hotel!"

As people continue to answer, we notice that we cover a lot of ground as a group, balanced in planners and nonplanners, strategists and muscle, risk-takers and overthinkers—if anyone is planning a future heist, give me a call because I have just the crew for you.

We transition to the dinner table, and as the dinner gods would have it, Jane and Sarah are seated next to each other. Throughout the evening, their opposites-attract dynamic continues, dismayed by each other's responses, a stark contrast in perspective, approach, or reflection in every story and insight they share. I'm privately getting a good internal laugh at watching Jane's face in response to every story Sarah tells—at one point, she even exclaims, "I can't *imagine* what it's like to be you!" not in a judgmental way, but simply in pure amazement. Their interactions are charming and hilarious to witness, these two women with such different outlooks, personalities, and approaches to their lives.

Eventually, the group starts answering the question, "What has been a turning point in your life?" and Jane shares that her ex-husband was the man who took care of everything; he was The Man of the House, doting on her, *taking care of business* and the like. "I wanted for nothing and didn't have to make any decisions;

he did everything for us and our family." She then shares that he suffered a traumatic brain injury, never quite recovering, and that their relationship couldn't survive it. He wasn't the same—there were major changes in his personality and memory, and he abruptly wanted to start a new life without her. "That's when I realized that there is so much outside of our control, and so I try to gain as much foresight as possible, plan for what I can, because you never know what's going to happen to you." Her answer to the heist question from before came into clearer context, this developed skill of trying to forecast and plan whatever she can.

Next Sarah shares, "A turning point for me was when I finally started sharing about my childhood with my loved ones only a few years ago. I started going to therapy and began processing the effects from being abused as a child. I survived the unimaginable, my sister and I actually, we survived somehow… I got married when I was twenty-two to the most amazing man, but I didn't tell him any of this until I was forty. I'm just now seeing how sharing not only about my trauma, but about survival, about creating a beautiful life, about the life you can have after that amount of violence, could change people's lives and give them hope. There is so much freedom in sharing what you've been through."

It feels like the whole table is breathing in unison, collectively in awe at the story we've just heard, enraptured by both the heaviness of the details and the warmth that Sarah brings to each word. She shares more about her childhood, and the people who helped her get out of the unimaginable abuse she was experiencing, find safe adults to live with, and the other milestones along the way that have shaped who she is now.

I find it fascinating that both Sarah and Jane have these powerful stories of trial and heartbreak, of starting over with resilience and determination, and *completely* different conclusions and responses from those experiences. Jane responded to her world being turned upside down by becoming vigilant, intentional, and always having a plan (and a backup, and a backup for the backup…); Sarah concluded that there is almost nothing that we can control, so why control anything? We have this stark contrast of two women who have walked fearlessly into their lives, sitting next to each other at the table as the clearest representation of different sides of the same coin that you could possibly see.

As I start to write this essay, I email Sarah and Jane to get their reflections on the night. It feels fitting that Jane writes me back right away with a few time slots that work for her in between weekend pickleball and salsa dancing. "I like to keep a busy social calendar," she says when we chat on a bright Sunday afternoon. It feels equally fitting that Sarah didn't write me back, out there floating around in the world, free from and unburdened by inboxes and debriefs.

Jane remarks that it really stood out to her when I said that everyone who's meant to be at dinner that night was there, especially given how the night unfolded. I ask her about her initial assessment of Sarah, and she says, "You know, at first, I hate to admit it, but initially I was so shocked by her persona that I thought, *Oh, this is the last person I'd want to sit next to at dinner. I hope I'm not sitting next to her at the table.* I was a bit peeved to see our names beside each other. And then as the night went on, I realized how fascinating it was to sit next to someone that I am the complete opposite of for the night. I thought, you know, in another universe, I could've turned out like her. Maybe there's a possibility that I could've been more of a free spirit."

Also from Jane: "I mean, REALLY. She drove all the way from Pennsylvania and DIDN'T BOOK A HOTEL!?!? I could never. But I suppose it's true: There *are* a lot of hotels in Toronto!!" Her ongoing shock at this really makes me laugh.

Isn't that the magic of being on this weird planet with this strange existence: that we are all made up of different strengths and preferences as ways of going about our lives, that we can go through similar things and come to completely different conclusions about the way things are, and that we can learn from each other's different approaches, which doesn't mean we have to change anything about the way we live our lives. We can witness each other's stories, allow ourselves to be moved by them, and not be moved to change our perspective or the way we would've responded in another person's circumstances.

I doubt Jane will ever go on an impromptu road trip somewhere ten hours away without booking a hotel. I doubt Sarah will adopt some sort of in-depth scheduling regimen for herself. *A spreadsheet?* Sarah would never. And the unique beauty of sharing a meal together at Dinner With Strangers was that these two women, who otherwise would most likely never cross paths, got to sit next to each other, see themselves in each other's stories, appreciate a completely different way of living, and continue on afterward as they were before.

This is how I invite us all to find our seats at the table together: to listen deeply to the stories of others, simply so that we can understand what it is like to walk the road that they are walking in the way they are walking it. We don't have to come to the same conclusions. We don't even have to agree on a single thing. Our only task is to see the humanity within the story, which is to say that we need to see the humanity within each other.

11

Does Baring Your Soul in Front of a Group of Strangers Count as Community?

Connection Is a Many-Layered Thing

I'm staring down the barrel of this book deadline, and after twelve hours of writing (with many breaks for meandering down to the kitchen for a snack and a fresh mug of tea, and the chime-y alarm on my phone that goes off every forty-five minutes to remind me to stand up, roll my shoulders, adjust my posture, and take five deep breaths), I get out of my sweats, put on some "real pants" and some mascara, and walk ten minutes to a restaurant for my friend Al's birthday. Out of the seven people at the table, I know only Al and his girlfriend, Amanda. They hug me when I arrive and ask how I'm doing, and I stare at them wide-eyed and tongue-tied in response. "In the thick of it!" I say, unsure where I should, or even could, start to give any kind of accurate or in-depth update on my current mental state or the thoughts rattling around my brain. They turn to the table to introduce me to their friends, and Amanda declares proudly, "Jess is writing a BOOK! She's going to be a published AUTHOR!" Everyone oohs and aahs a bit at that. I feel shy, and also, because I'm so tapped out, I don't particularly want to get into *the whole thing* of Dinner With Strangers, which tends to evoke a lot of questions.

It's truly incredible that I've built this dinner that people are fascinated by, and I know that it's totally crazy that my job is what it is. I have an increasingly unconventional life. And my little introvert self doesn't always want to talk about it, walk people through it, tell the whole story. I always particularly struggle with how to divert from talking about my work while around people who know me, that it might come off as false modesty, when really I just don't want the spotlight on me in any way. I've been in my book for the last twelve hours, and talking about it with strangers feels equal parts tender and exhausting.

I say the book is about the dinner series I run, and their friend Phil says, "Oh, Al's told me about you! So it's like a dating thing." "No, it's not for dating." "But it IS for single people, right?" "No, it's not specifically for singles. It's—" "So I guess it's like a networking thing?" "No, it's kind of anti-networking. It's actually—" "So does everyone come in pairs or they have to come alone?" "Almost everyone comes alone, yeah." "But it's a club, like a monthly thing? And people come back?" "No. Well, I've had repeat guests before, but it's always 98 percent new people at every dinner…"

This is going well, clearly.

Refining the elevator pitch for this project has come with time, and when we started talking about turning it into a business, Ryan and I would always get stumped about how we could describe what the "deliverables" were for the dinner. People would ask (and continue to ask), "Okay, but what's the point of this?" It is apparently not an enticing sales pitch to say, "The point is simply to gather with strangers, share some stories, and see what unfolds." The format is always the same, but each dinner has its own unique magic depending on who is around the table. Even if we were to ask exactly the same questions at every single dinner, the conversation and experience would be completely different because of the way every person would answer each question so differently. Some dinners have been full of natural storytellers and are fascinating and entertaining. Some are gentle, subdued, and heartfelt. Some are particularly philosophical and heady. Some have a table full of people who are similar in age, or more parents than not parents, and sometimes it's as if we've cast the whole thing with the most opposite people in the world. No one needs to become best friends—we aren't solving anything, and we aren't expecting lasting connections to form, or for anyone to find their next business partner.

Nine years in, and I'm still switching up how exactly I define *the point* of all this.

After relaunching in 2023, I notice that at each dinner, someone inevitably says, "Wow, this is like group therapy!" and everyone laughs. This always unsettles me; I'm not trying to or pretending to be a therapist. Therapy happens with the guidance of trained professionals. People share about their lives, or a recent insight or breakthrough, and sometimes they speak up after someone else shares and they say, "I've gone through something similar," or, "Take it from me, you're going to be all right," or, "Let's talk after dinner—I might know someone who can help you with that," or, "That was so inspiring." I could go on. People who have never met before, being moved by each other.

After one dinner in particular (very breakthrough-heavy, lots of *this is like group therapy* comparisons being thrown around among guests), I bring it up to Riley, who's been cheffing for the last six dinners. "It makes me so uncomfortable! Why does it get under my skin like this?!" I say, still stumped at the correlation. "We're just sharing! We're telling stories, which of course are tender and vulnerable and real, but it's not *therapy*." Riley thinks for a minute, wiping down the stove as we have a post-dinner debrief and beer at the kitchen island. "No, it's *not* therapy…but it *is* therapeutic." I like his spin on it, mulling it over a bit in my mind. Maybe it's therapeutic like the way people talk about how they feel after going for a run. Like scheduling a good cry in the shower (what, you don't schedule your cries sometimes?). Like a long walk with a friend. I can get on board with *therapeutic,* I suppose.

One day I'm catching up with my friend Allie, who is a psychologist—an *actual* professional in the therapy space. I bring up this "group therapy" comment pattern I've been hearing to get her take on it. She pauses for a second before saying, "You know what

I think it is? Therapy is more or less the only place where most people share how they're *really* doing… It's one of the only places that most people actually show up as themselves, without masks, and talk with someone who's invested and interested in what they have to say. So they're equating, or at least comparing, Dinner With Strangers to therapy because they're not used to sharing in this way anywhere else."

I only know how *I* have conversations, which is ideally and often reflecting on the abyss of feelings I have, and being curious about everyone else's personal abyss. I forget that I have a particular desire to share about what worries us, what we're dreaming up, how we're *actually* doing, which can come off as intense, serious, or even intrusive at times. That's the way Ryan and I talk to each other, hence why we have no concept of a *quick catch-up* over coffee. There are only four-plus-hours-long brunches. There is only solving most of the world's problems over a bottle of wine and splitting a burger at The Comrade in Leslieville. Maybe even to a fault, during any interaction, I am hoping that the conversation *goes somewhere.* Are we really going to go an entire night and only talk about our bitchy coworker, the jeans we just bought, the show we just watched, and not how we're feeling inside of our lives?

I don't want it to be an anomaly to greet each other with earnestness and curiosity, and to respond with vulnerability. And yet repeatedly, while at dinner with twenty strangers, people take the opportunity as the first time they open up about the quiet dream they've been secretly holding, or the first time they say out loud that they're not really sure what they're looking for, or the first time in a long time that they tell a story about their brother. I'm grateful whenever this happens, and that people feel safe to share these things at dinner. I wonder how much of this is simply about how maxed out and busy we all feel, how taxed we are, how there is so much noise and muchness and pressure to partake and keep up. We're mostly trying to get from sunup to sundown. I also know that there are plenty of questions I don't want to be asked because I know that once I say the answer out loud, then I'd have to do something about it, and that *something* can feel like tugging at the one thread that will unravel the entire sweater. If the sweater goes, what will we cover ourselves with next?

Is it too big of a question to ask ourselves how many places (if any) we are able to be honest about who and where we are? Is it too big of a question to ask how often we are honest with ourselves?

———

I have been wrestling with whether or not this project is *building community*. Even though I host dinners upward of twice a month, it's 98 percent a new group every time, so we're hitting reset on the experience with every dinner. It's not like a yoga studio or a book club or a weekly meet-up where everyone's seeing the same people on a regular basis, building on their connections each time. I wonder if it's *building community* insofar as guests are experiencing and practicing a fresh way of interacting, asking an intentional question, listening to every person in the room answer, and seeing how impactful that can be, and then maybe bringing that practice back to the communities they're already a part of.

I'm facilitating an online workshop on "cultivating a compassionate inner voice," and today's module is on treating ourselves like we would a friend. Many of the participants I've known for years—dedicated and supportive people within my writing community who have participated in many workshops and online classes. This is a community in the way that we've gotten to know each other through our writing and through meeting regularly. Friendships have formed. Cards and letters are regularly sent. Multiple people are editing each other's poetry book manuscripts. They meet up when they're in each other's city. Elizabeth announced her first pregnancy at the beginning of Poetry Club last summer, and now sweet Jonas is here, usually making a cameo during our workshops at some point, his bright, twinkly eyes staring intently at our weird floating heads on the Zoom screen. We learn of Kate's daughter's cancer, and people send cards and collect poems about hope and uncertainty and motherhood. They write a collective poem and surprise her with it in the mail.

During the inner voice workshop, I ask people to share about a time a friend has shown up for them, and Sam shares about how her friend Cierra lent her car to Sam for six months last year. "Cierra lives walking distance to her work, so she just handed me the keys, and my car troubles just kept snowballing so that it took that long to get them sorted. And people around town were increasingly puzzled, like, *you're still driving your friend's car?* But that's the kind of friendship group we have. We help each other out. We *rely* on each other." The online group marvels at the generosity, and how beautiful it is that Sam has that kind of network. She continues, "When I first started dating JJ, he needed extra hands for a gig he was doing, and I said, 'Oh, why don't I text the crew and see if anyone is free on Tuesday?' JJ was uncomfortable with that, didn't want to come off as needy, wondered if it was overstepping, and I said, 'We've created an environment where asking for that is not a big deal.'"

Sam's ecosystem of support inspires us all deeply, some to the point of tears. We marvel at what it's like to have the kind of support around you where the care isn't in any way transactional; there's no keeping score. Friends show up for each other in count-less, continual, immeasurable ways: from check-ins to going to doctor's appointments together to making dinner for each other to watching each other's kids when you *literally can't even* to sitting next to each other when someone has to make a difficult phone call to helping someone with their post-surgery incision cleaning so their mom doesn't have to do it to coming over while you fold laundry because laundry is less menial with a good chitchat accom-panying it.

We talk about how difficult it can be to ask for help, espe-cially when it feels like we're in need more than others, or more than usual. We discuss why it feels like there's a difference between being *in need* and being *needy*—a mysterious, elusive barometer of crossing over to being a "burden" that is very NOT OKAY in society. Likewise, we often know how to swoop in and rally when the worst happens: When a natural disaster hits, we donate diapers and cash and invite people into our homes to recover or while they sort themselves out. When a personal disaster hits, we organize food trains and bring flowers and offer our time and resources. And then the dust settles, and we forget that the ripple effects of disaster can be felt for a lifetime. The needs may become less acute, but the recovery lingers on.

What if we learned how to ask for support, even if it's not a crisis-level disaster? What if we're in a weird mood and just want to vent, or we have a really bad cold that isn't life-threatening but it would feel really crappy to walk to the pharmacy for cold medicine, so maybe a friend could do a run for sick supplies on our behalf? What if we interact with the understanding that having needs and wants is so incredibly *human* of us, and part of being human is wanting to not do it all alone? What if part of being human is real-izing that we *can't* do it all alone?

Ryan and I are hosting our first dinner back at the hair studio after COVID restrictions have lifted. We ask the table, "How is your life different from a year ago?" and Jay shares that he and his wife have decided to separate after seventeen years together, but because they both have parents with complicated health issues going on right now, they haven't told their families that they're in the process of filing for divorce. They still want to support each other through this season of uncertainty, and they don't want to make it weird for their families, who might be confused about why they're making hospital visits together when they just said they're getting divorced. They've each told only a single friend, in fact, not ready to start the process of sharing with their circle at large and the possible emotional reactions from their very tight-knit group. "It feels so good to be able to talk about this here, honestly," he says. "The irony of being able to be the most honest with a room full of strangers isn't lost on me. In a way, you all know the truest version of me right now, because the people who know me best don't know this very big thing."

Jay's story inspires Dylan to share about the shifts he's processing too. "I'm a pastor, and my family and I even live in a house that is owned by the church I work at. And…I'm having a crisis of faith of sorts." He hesitates. "Is it a crisis? I don't know. I still believe in God…It's just…I'm processing a lot. And my views on a lot of things have shifted, and shifted out of line with the tenets of our particular church. So I'm having this personal revelation, which is intrinsically tied to my job, and intrinsically tied to my living situation. My best friend, whom I would usually talk to about anything personal, is my *boss*—the head pastor of our church. So I can't exactly talk to him about all of this. It feels oddly comforting to share with all of you how I'm actually doing, and what I'm actually going through, which ironically I feel unable to do with people who know me best."

Jay and Dylan are able to share so freely with the table precisely because we aren't intertwined in their close communities. We have no skin in the game. Our feelings aren't hurt and our lives are not affected in the slightest by their stories, other than simply being empathetic to both of their situations. We as strangers are able to be overwhelmingly objective. After dinner, we also will go back to our usual lives, not assuming any responsibility to check in or follow up or see how we can support Jay or Dylan if we don't want to stay in touch.

If the loosest definition of community is showing up for each other, then coming to a dinner where you share with strangers and listen to strangers and eat with strangers is a facet of community. Listening to Jay and Dylan and being able to say "That sounds really hard. I'm glad you feel like you can share fully and honestly here" is a facet of community. Noticing that my neighbors haven't shoveled their sidewalk after the insane snowstorm last week, and rather than rolling my eyes and assuming they're lazy, instead just getting my shovel and taking fifteen minutes to do it myself, because maybe they're away or maybe they're sick or maybe someone sprained their ankle or maybe it's none of my business and I have the time and ability to do it, is a facet of community. My best friend texting me "Happy birthday, Gus!" on my nephew's birthday is a facet of community—she cares about my nephew because I care about my nephew. Running home for a few bucks and going back to the lemonade stand that the kids four houses down have set up is a facet of community (buying lemonade at a kid's front yard lemonade stand is mandatory actually—sorry, I don't make the rules).

Learning the names of the workers at the local butcher and coffee shop and bar is a facet of community. Volunteering at your kid's school for Popsicle Day is a facet of community. Volunteering to be someone's emergency contact is a facet of community. Sparing a few minutes is a facet of community. Going out of your way for someone in any way is a facet of community. Committing to and investing in the place that we live and the spaces we frequent and the people we encounter is a facet of community. Inviting people to know us is a facet of community.

Dinner With Strangers is proof that we don't have to know each other long (or at all) in order to show up for each other in some way; if we see an opportunity to offer what we have in a time of need, may we not hesitate to do so. Each facet of care and attention and offering is a way that we participate in taking care of each other, whether we know each other's names or not, have each other's phone numbers or not, whether we're in regular communication with each other or not.

Together, those facets create an ecosystem. Maybe we call that ecosystem a community.

12

Introvert Walks into a Room

Connection Is for Everyone,
Even When It Drains You

It's December 2017. I'm at my boyfriend Rashid's college friend's holiday party, hosted in the party room of their building. It's a potluck—folding tables and festive red tablecloths deployed to welcome the vast reaches of this social web to which I am connected only via girlfriendom. Rashid has made some sort of delicious braised duck situation that he's very excited about. For my part, I've brought two bottles of cab franc with a funky label (as good a reason as any to buy a bottle of wine): It displays a man juggling many things while balancing on a ball. The ball is balancing on an elephant's trunk. The elephant is riding a tiny bicycle. Perhaps the man has a cartoon mustache or maybe I am making that up. Perhaps they know what it feels like to try to stay upright and really try not to break an ankle while holding so much all at once.

Rashid knows a good handful of people at the holiday party—thirty or so McGill University grads with neuroscience-adjacent degrees, many of whom he hasn't seen in a while. I, a Poster Child Introvert, am strapped in for a holiday party with a bunch of people I don't know. I've given myself plenty of pep talks to get in the right headspace for a social situation such as this. Rashid and I are deeply in love but ever increasingly in a precarious place in our relationship, so I'm feeling an added layer of (self-inflicted) pressure for the night to go well—which is a way to say I want *us* to go well—along with an added dread that I'm not particularly *in the mood* to be extra bubbly and bright in a room full of strangers.

People are often surprised to find out that I'm an introvert—a full-blown, far-side-of-the-spectrum introvert, in fact, not even an *extroverted* introvert. Left to my own devices, I think I'm in my truest nature while spending hours deep diving into the pool of my internal world, puttering and pondering, imagining, daydreaming, mulling an idea over in my head like palming a stone plucked out of a river. It can be difficult to draw me out of myself, and it can be exhausting to override this desire to go inward if neglected for too long.

That being said, I am also deeply curious about people and absolutely comfortable in front of crowds and on stages. I am often the last to leave events when I feel engaged in conversations and feel at ease with the people I'm with—it just results in a full-body depression the next day, battery completely zapped, even if I had the best time of my life the night before.

Social situations feel stressful to me when I feel like I have to overfunction in a different demeanor than feels natural. There are certain social situations where I feel anxious (usually when meeting new people, before we find a steady flow of conversation), and then even when I'm with people I know really well, I may feel like I need to tap into the backup reserve of social energy if it's been a busy week or I'm particularly deep into my internal world. Some (most? many?) introverts might not feel the same pressure to engage how people want them to engage, but while I would sometimes rather keep to myself and be left to my daydreaming and observation from the shadows, I am *also* not content to stand quietly in the corner in the company of my own thoughts regardless of what other partygoers might think of me doing so. I care that they might be uncomfortable or weirded out or concerned about my quietness, and so I do an insane amount of mental gymnastics to deliver what I think people need from me. I walk into a room and immediately assess *What does everyone—anyone—want from me? Who do they need me to be?*

I'm not sure when this image first arrived to me, but when I feel the call to overfunction arise, I picture myself as the dancing frog with the top hat from Warner Bros. I see in my mind's eye a bunch of hats lined up on a stage, each labeled with a different demeanor: charming / aloof / rambling / sarcastic / pithy / sweet / flirty / inquisitive / entertaining. These many chapeaus are ready to be plucked up and put on to give whoever I'm talking to what I think they want from me. So when Rashid and I head out to the party, I am sure to bring my extensive hat collection along.

We make it to the party room and make our way through a few intros, and I stay mostly glued to Rashid as I get my social bearings and assess which top hat the room requires of me. When it's time to eat, we join the line in front of the makeshift buffet, everyone's festive dishes offered in their post-college Pyrexes and Crock-Pots. We fill our plates. I head to the table, expecting Rashid to be right behind me, but he gets held up saying hi to someone who just arrived. I sit myself down at the emptier side of the table, and before I know it, two people sit down on either side of me. *Oh no, oh god,* I think. I consider letting them know I'm saving a seat for my Emotional Support Extrovert Boyfriend, but I decide, hello, I'm an adult; I'm an adult with social capabilities; I'm an adult who's just recently started a weird dinner series in my friend's hair studio where I talk to strangers all the time. I can sit next to these very nice people and have a perfectly pleasant time, surely. Rashid catches my eye on his way to the other side of the table, and I communicate in our secret eyeball language that I'm totally good and fine and capable and mature and comfortable and fine (I'm *fine*). Obviously. We both shrug, and he sits down directly across from me, twenty-ish people away, and we embark on the experience of eating food at a table with many people.

The woman to my right just moved downtown a few months ago from the suburbs and she's *so excited about Christmas baking*. I say genuinely that I am in awe of bakers, as I am not patient or meticulous. She is slightly disappointed that I don't have a favorite Christmas cookie (how does one choose?). She is disappointed in my lack of knowledge of Hallmark movies, recent or canonical. I offer a few anecdotes on my own holiday traditions. We marvel at our different Christmas interests and motivations. I've got about two to three more Christmas tidbits in me before hitting my maximum capacity.

The dinner guest to my left is *in bitcoin*. It's 2017, so bitcoin is especially new. I decide that I will take the opportunity of this seating arrangement to educate myself on *what's up with this whole crypto thing*. Please explain it to me like I'm five. He obliges in an informative, clear, non-mansplaining tone. I decide that he should teach bitcoin for kindergartners. I feel like I'm doing a great job of asking engaging questions while tracking (I think) what he's talking about. I look at Rashid at the opposite end of the table—fully engaged in the conversation he's having, nodding emphatically at what his friend is saying and talking with grand hand gestures in the way he does when he's really leaning into the dramatics of whatever story he's telling—and I experience one of my favorite feelings in the world: seeing the person I love looking at ease and happy across the room from me. Like: Wow, there's my favorite person, having a good time. I feel proud that, should he look up and see me, he might feel the same way, maybe seeing me look pensive and wise as I nod emphatically and obtain a brand-new understanding of the blockchain.

My Easy-Breezy, Engaged Party Guest–labeled top hat sits like a crown on my head. I'm making it through this conversation successfully (most of being an introvert at a party is sitting there asking yourself, *Am I doing well being a nice, charming human at a party? Yes, I am* or *Oh no, oh crap, I'm not,* over and over again). Our plates are nearly empty. Crypto Dude and I briefly make it on to a different topic, and then guests are starting to shuffle around and mix up the seating arrangement. A stranger to me but a familiar friend to Crypto Dude slaps him on the back and says, "Man! How's it going being a crypto dude?!" And I think to myself, *Self, you've done it, you've done enough, you've heard probably the most you'll ever hear or retain about crypto, you simply cannot and do not need to hit restart on this conversation.* I offer New Guy my seat and head over to Rashid and his dinner companion, put my arms around both of them, and say, "What are we talking about over here?" They both laugh, deep in conversation about the merits of nihilism and the meaninglessness of *all this living stuff* and whether life's pointlessness is exactly the reason we should try to care about being good humans. "You know, light dinner chat," they say. I dramatically pull up a chair in relief, saying, "Now *this* is a conversation I can deep dive into immediately!" I'm relieved to be back in existential territory with at least one familiar person. We chat with ease about the unknowable mysteries of the universe over dessert.

—

I'm really putting the magnifying glass up to how I feel in social situations, considering what makes them feel incredibly draining at times and why; what feels inspiring, engaging, and maybe even *fun*; and what are components are that might tip an interaction one way or the other. I'm trying to decipher what's related to introversion and what is actually related to demeanor and personality (to what degree someone is shy or sociable or bubbly or outgoing or gregarious or low-key), general anxiety, codependence, implicit and unexamined social conditioning, or something else entirely. We generally think of quiet, reserved people as introverts, when truly introversion and extroversion aren't about behavior; they're about how we recharge our social battery. We also largely perceive extroverts as *those who like being around people* and introverts as *those who do NOT like being around people.* In reality, we are all social, relational creatures who thrive in community and wither in isolation. I speak for *my kind* when I say that we genuinely want to connect in a meaningful way, which I think is a universal desire. "Meaningful" simply looks different to each of us, just as our interests, priorities, and capacities vary. So the anxiety I feel when meeting someone new isn't the mere fact that I'm engaging with someone and that in and of itself is a drag for me; the anxiety comes from being unsure who's going to carry the conversation and for how long. It comes from wanting mutual presence and engagement. It comes from the self-consciousness that maybe I'm *too much* for some people. I want to find a way to converse that feels like we're connecting, not just like we're handing a topical conversation hot potato between us. I am deeply craving for us to *be ourselves,* by which I mean in any manner of ways sharing what our personal human existence is like. And yet, because that is, I recognize, *intense,* I often wait for the other person to signal that deep, heady, existential Jess is invited and welcome to the conversation.

I recently tapped into my online audience's wisdom on this topic, asking introverts and extroverts alike to share about their experiences and interpretations on the topic—what exhausts them and energizes them, what they feel people often misunderstand about them, and how they feel about small talk. What surprised me most was how overwhelmingly introverts expressed that people often assume that they don't want to connect at all when, in fact, they want to connect deeply but might not know how to initiate that kind of connection. And extroverts overwhelmingly expressed that, despite popular belief, they don't like conversations that stay surface level, but they might not know how to take the conversation to a deeper level. They also expressed how disappointing it can feel when introverts seem disengaged or unwilling to try to find a rhythm to the conversation.

As an attempt to distill some "official" data or insight from this (casual) research, I'd venture to say that we collectively are looking for meaningful connections, and we all have different ways of getting there. It's disappointing when people seem disinterested in engaging with us, and there are so many reasons why someone might be having a difficult time doing so on any particular day. It feels great to have someone show genuine interest in getting to know us, and generous, genuine interest is something that both introverts and extroverts are capable of practicing.

———

With my introversion in mind, Dinner With Strangers is structured to be introvert-friendly: The "activities" for the night are dependable and consistent, laid out ahead of time so guests will have an understanding of what they're signing up for. It's built to immediately sidestep empty small talk but still utilizes absolutely vital icebreaker questions to start the night—without them, the deeper conversations wouldn't be possible. Yet even with the approachable icebreaker questions, we subliminally pose the question *what does it feel like to be you?* at every point of the dinner.

Dinner With Strangers invites people to connect in the way that I like to connect with people (when I feel like I'm in the mood to connect with people). It encourages and challenges each guest to examine the kinds of conversations they're having and what questions they're asking each other and hopefully offers tools and inspiration to create more moments of connection with strangers and friends alike.

———

I'm taking myself out for dinner in Vancouver's West End after a long day of writing. I've had a long, glorious week of peopleing with some of the people who know me best, right before the Christmas holidays. I told myself I'd get so much writing done this week in this ideal setting—escaping the harsher winter weather of Toronto as an added bonus, looking for inspiration and calm in the landscape I grew up in: misty mornings walking the inlet and smelling the pine and the salty air envelop me in their unhurried steadiness.

I'll take all the inspiration I can get—the first nine chapters of this book are due on Monday, and I'm feeling behind and rushed and nervous to get my first bout of feedback from my editor. Of course in reality, the output is slow and I've struggled with boundaries around time management and I haven't been able to sink into my creative world when I do sneak off to write in between having coffee dates and catching up over dinner and teaching my one-and-a-half-year-old nephew how to really get the most noise possible out of the harmonica I gifted him for Christmas. So instead of staying at my parents' as I intended, I've sent myself on a timeout in downtown Vancouver to hermit and pour into my work. I've loved the social week I've had, and I desperately want to be alone.

I walk down Denman Street and into a little Italian spot with the intention of having a leisurely, anonymous dinner armed with a novel tucked under my arm to send the message that I'd like to keep to myself, no need to worry about or entertain me, I've got Sally Rooney's latest novel for that!

The host tells me any open seat at the bar is mine, and I survey my potential neighbors for the most inconspicuous ones. On the far end: a couple who seem boisterous; they're talking loudly and actively looking around the room. Three empty seats and then a second couple, a little more unobtrusive, just finishing their dinner. On the short end of the bar: two empty seats and the evidence of a solo diner who is currently in the bathroom. I take my chances and sit on the short end of the bar in between the second couple and the mystery solo diner.

Within minutes, I can tell that every single person involved in this dining arrangement is part of a colorful cast of characters, including our bartender, who is in his mid-forties, tatted up to his earlobes and down to his fingertips. I know even before he confirms it an hour and a half later that he's definitely in a band of some sort. As he makes an order of cappuccinos, he's dancing and turning the espresso machine knobs like he's playing the wildest DJ set of his life. The way he's engaging each person at the bar, it's clear that he is an interactive, social bartender, which I definitely appreciate and usually love as a solo diner, but I'm so peopled out and reflectioned out that I don't want to extrovert any inch beyond ordering my food and a glass of chenin blanc.

The solo diner returns to her seat, and I immediately recognize that she is there to see and be seen, loudly inserting herself into various conversations around her and lingering in them regardless of the implicit (or explicit) social cues that people aren't loving her contributions. She's saying hi to every staff member who walks past her, reaching out far past her chair to graze their elbow if any of them avert their eyes (and many do), calling them each by name, clear that she's been there a lot, has been making an effort to become a regular, and perhaps has also overstayed her welcome a time or two, already slurring her words a bit while she reaches for her wineglass. "Yeah, I'm back again; crazy, right?!" She keeps saying to them, "I just have to crawl up the stairs to the apartment above us when I stumble home!" Compassionately, I can pretty safely assume she's lonely, maybe not just here in Vancouver but in her life at large. Personally, my social battery is blinking on empty, making me incredibly resistant to engage in Her Whole Thing if at all possible.

Someone drops off her charred salmon and asks if she'd like another glass of wine, and she says, "*Andrew* really likes to pick out my wine for me actually." (I'm sure he does.) She tries with all her might to start up a conversation with the couple to the right of me (I'm sitting directly in between her line of contact), interjecting whenever Andrew The Bartender starts bantering with them, and they're politely responding to her quips before returning to their own conversation. I slump deeper into my seat, head lowered to a dramatic level, physically closing off the possibility of someone catching my eye to initiate contact. I've made a pact with myself that I am *introverting* tonight, damn it! I will not imbibe with the chatty bartender and the showy regular.

Five minutes after I sit down, the boisterous couple from the far end of the bar is on their way out the door, and the man taps me on the shoulder, looks me up and down, and says in a shocked, mesmerized-but-in-a-slimy-way tone, "Wow, you really never see people reading anymore. How *fascinating*. I *must* know your name." (It's always nice to surprise and delight people with such unique overachievements as literacy; I'm glad I can serve as an inspiration.) His wife smiles at me tensely. I introduce myself to them for her sake, and he pretends he's heard of the author of the book I'm reading, says again how amazing it is to see someone *reading in real life*. I die a thousand introvert deaths in the span of our forty-five-second interaction, briefly catching the eye of the other couple at the bar, who both give me an eyebrow raise in solidarity. Our baffled couple leaves, and I let out a sigh, but not wanting to get our solo friend involved in a debrief, I go back to my book.

The remaining couple has ordered various rounds of aperitifs, starting with amaro and then moving on to Cynar (an Italian amaro), which the bartender remarks sounds like a word in Chinese. The wife and the bartender then discuss various words in Chinese that sound similar to the Western ear but have very different meanings. Discuss the merits of aperitifs and digestifs in various cultures (the French and their pastis and absinthes, the Italians and their amaros, the Greeks and their sambuca, it goes on and on), and the bartender talks the couple into ordering some green Chartreuse—an herbaceous, sweet liqueur made by monks in the French countryside. The couple loves it, making jokes about monks needing to direct their time and attention to anything other than matters of love and romance; of course it's good. Our solo diner covets their rapt attention from Andrew, and after a few failed attempts of talking over my head about monks and herbs and liqueurs on ice or not on ice, she says, "Andrew, *I* want a green Chartreuse too." Andrew is hesitant. "Are you sure? It's really strong." "I'm sure! It seems so *fun*." "Well, how about a taster?" Andrew hands her a splash of Chartreuse in a thimble-size glass and silently slides *me* one as well. I have now reached the furthest limits of my refusal to engage, being invited into the fold of the socialization of this corner of the bar. An offering like an olive branch, or maybe like a dare, who's to say. I succumb, finally, to the social situation at hand, lifting my little thimble, a chartreuse-colored white flag. *Here we go, I guess; let's see what happens,* I think to myself.

The man from the couple beside me says, "Ah, I was wondering what would be strong enough to pull you out of your book! Turns out the monks have what it takes!" He asks if I'm from Vancouver, and I say I'm just visiting the city, downtown for work. When he asks what I do, I consider lying. As I say in my intro spiel at every Dinner With Strangers: If you're someone who's going through something—whether exciting or serious or heavy—and for tonight, you want to give yourself a break from your life at this table of strangers and be the person who's *not* going through that thing, we'll respect your vagueness. Do what you need.

I do divulge that I'm a writer, and without skipping a beat, he responds, "Oh! A psychic told me just last week that I should write a book!" I'm amused by his response (and amused that this is overwhelmingly people's response when you tell them that you're writing a book—minus the psychic part), relieved that perhaps I will, in fact, get away with not talking about my work at all—my preferred outcome for the evening. When I inquire if he's a writer, he says, "Not even!" So I ask, "Well, what would your book be about?" and he sits back a minute before saying, "Spirituality.

Spirituality as a door to yourself." I lean in, can't help it. If someone's going to interrupt my silent dining experience, they'd better lead with a topic like this.

He shares that he spent most of his twenties looking for God "or something like it" by way of psychedelic drugs and at parties and in music and "all that hippie shit" before developing a devoted practice in multiple forms of martial arts. "First I tried to unravel from any confines and all structure from my childhood, trying to free myself through complete abandon. Complete oblivion in a way. And then swung the other way completely, diving into discipline, devotion, and trying to desperately prove…I don't know, something. That I was *man* enough maybe, whatever that actually means. And ultimately I found that there is no way, no direction, no path, except going inwards, discovering yourself as you are, independent of the expectations that the world puts on you. We are our own guides. We hold our own answers."

I have a good internal laugh at the fact that the very ethos of my business has come to fruition the second I engage with the people around me. I put my desire to hermit aside, and the couple and I continue to talk for the next thirty minutes about turning points in our lives, our experiences with religion and spirituality, even swapping our favorite Buddhist parables that we keep tucked close to our chests. I share about Dinner With Strangers and the book I'm trying to write. Our solo diner friend chimes in a few times before getting bored with our conversation and moving on to other patrons in the restaurant.

I finish my wine and ask for my bill, grateful for the way the night ended up and confused by what to make of the potential takeaway here. I was trying to honor my maxed-out social battery. I was attempting to practice some self-care by having a night out in a city where no one knows me, hoping to fly under the radar from the rest of humanity and head to bed early. I was met with an inspiring, thought-provoking conversation once I did open myself up to the conversation—an excellent feather in the cap of my work's ethos. I don't owe anyone access to my time or my inner world, but when we can connect on something meaningful and true, I'm always glad to go there.

Just as I'm leaving the restaurant, my phone buzzes and someone texts me that he's finished work and is a few blocks away. This person is what the mystics would probably describe as a twin flame—my mirrored self in many ways, evident from the minute we met that there's something mysterious and intertwined and allegorical about why we crashed into each other's lives. Or maybe it's simply that we're two deep-feeling, sometimes manically dreaming, complexly avoidant artist types that can't get it together enough to be anything other than people who care a whole lot about the other and aren't sure what (if anything) to do with that. Either way, despite my absolutely fried nervous system and the craziness of the last two hours, I find myself walking into a bar on the outskirts of Gastown at 11:45 p.m., and we spend another four hours talking into the night. My cup, previously completely empty, is suddenly brimming over.

These days I am learning how to take care of my introvert battery. I try to show up as I am, even if that is subdued, withdrawn, or moody. I occasionally rely on my Top Hats of Overfunctioning in professional settings but otherwise try to leave them at home. I give myself grace when I can't find it within myself to emerge from the caverns of my inner world. I give myself permission to opt out when my reserves feel low. I schedule in wide swaths of recovery time after event days (no alarm, no schedule, absolutely no social plans no matter how fun they seem). I am careful to pay attention to how much time I'm spending by myself—prone to malaise, and a tendency to get more agitated the less time I spend with others, I remind myself that it's more than likely that I will be surprised, uplifted, and inspired by the simplest interactions, should I nudge myself out of my own head and out into the world around me.

One of the beautiful things about each of us being wired differently is that we get to take care of each other by offering the things that come naturally. Those who find it easy to start conversations help those who aren't sure how to initiate. Those who tend to hang back in conversation often have the most astute observations that enrich the conversation. The planners are often the glue of group chats, which lead to group hangs (thank god somebody has some foresight to make reservations and get us out of our house from time to time!). The overthinkers bring the conversation into complex hypotheticals that make us think, and the jokesters (and the peacekeepers) bring levity in their own ways in tense moments. We challenge, tend, protect, and strengthen each other just by showing up as we are.

The best way we can take care of *ourselves* is to tend to the unique and specific calibration of rest, reprieve, and reset that we personally need. Sometimes that looks like seeking comfort and sometimes that looks like nudging ourselves out of our comfort zone. Sometimes that looks like dancing it out with thousands of people at a concert, or turning the phone to silent and reading a book for eight hours, or going on a long walk with an old friend. It's paying attention to our reserves and our limits and not forcing ourselves to act a certain way out of obligation.

If there's any homework here, it's simply for each of us to get really clear on what we bring (to the table, you could say) and what we need. There are things we all benefit from: thoughtful questions, attentive listening, careful consideration of how those around us feel within the social situation, and what we might offer to make people feel included. And if you see a woman deeply absorbed in her book while eating a bowl of spaghetti, consider letting her be.

13

We Need to Hear More Love Stories

Expanding Our Understanding of Closeness

My friends are the loves of my life, and there's no convincing me otherwise. We're the first to know about bad dates and good ones, about what happened in the summer, and the reason I might have rolled my eyes at my mother yesterday. We hear about doubts and fears and the things we're afraid to say—they're the ones who tell me to say it anyway. They remind me who I am. They come over with snacks and flowers and those extra-gooey chocolate chip cookies that are perfectly semisweet from Le Gourmand even when I said I didn't want anything.

We sleep on each other's couches and in spare rooms; raid each other's fridges; sit for long hours on balconies sharing our secrets, confessing our sins, smoking the cigarettes we say we don't smoke; bring over laundry when the machine breaks; listen again to the story about their brothers. We know the arguments and petitions and expectations that others put on us. We know the dreams harbored in our heads. We know which soap scent to pick over the other one.

Once on a short visit back to Toronto from San Francisco, I sat in a sticky, dark bar with women who love me wholly, and I confessed my sadness and my dismay; my relationship was in shambles and I felt I was to blame. I told them I understood his frustration and disappointment, how difficult it must be to be with me, how difficult it must be to love me. Didn't Alexandra slam the table so loudly that it frightened the family sitting beside us. "But you are SO EASY to love!" she shouted at me, rattling something hopeful in me that I thought had died. "But my angst," I said, "but my indecision. But all the feelings that keep rising even though I should be glad, should be grateful, should be reasonable right now." But all the other things that were even harder to say.

She wouldn't hear it. There was only love, only insistence on what shines. Only the belief that someone might be so lucky to sit in the mystery with me while I march at its foundation again and again and again until some sort of resolve might arrive.

———

There is no relational expectation for Dinner With Strangers; no one is required to stay in touch, to make a new friend, or to even find anything in common with anyone else at the table. The only expectation is that people are open-minded to what may unfold in our conversation, that they are generous with their curiosity and with their listening, and honest, vulnerable, and humble in what they share. By its nature, it is ideal (and even necessary) that there is no desired or orchestrated outcome from each gathering. Because of this, we're able to witness each other freely and fully.

Most friendships start organically and without agenda as well—we generally don't go out in the world thinking, *I'm in the market for a new best friend, and a new best friend only. No other kinds of friendships for me right now, just this one specific kind of friend.* Like this: It's day one of preschool and Sophie offers me a crayon. We partner up, we play in the schoolyard, we sit next to each other at lunch, we ask our parents if we can play for the afternoon. Somewhere along the way, without discussing or negotiating or putting a name on it, we claim each other as friends. Somewhere it becomes understood that we will continually make plans to hang out. Along the way, we implicitly declare our loyalty to each other, whether through engaging in playground warfare or standing up to Cody after he makes fun of Sophie's adorable (admittedly cartoon-ish) glasses or when Kendra says my science fair project is lame (it *is* lame, Kendra, and I'm at peace with that). We write what we mean to each other explicitly in a birthday card or a note passed in class, but we haven't formally declared our friendship. We don't have a conversation about *what this is* or *where this is going* or if we're *good for one another.* We let the relationship emerge organically, allowing for the person to reveal themselves as they are, refraining from expectations that anyone will drastically change anything about their nature or personality or way of relating to us. From preschool onward, countless friendships have been forged without our being on the lookout for a specific structure or dynamic. They simply form as they're meant to.

And then, when it comes to dating, we throw all this out the window.

It took me a while to wrap my head around how to host a singles event in the Dinner With Strangers way. Since the beginning, the number one thing people have requested (read: insist on) at the end of any dinner is for me to host something specifically for singles. "This is such a great way to get to know people!" they say. "Dating is so hard!" "I'm sick of dating apps!" "Bring these questions to the dating scene!" While I'm familiar with the overall dating climate and have shared similar frustrations in my own life, I've been reluctant to host any kind of dating event; I'm doubtful, from a statistical perspective, what the odds would be that anyone would actually hit it off with someone else romantically at a twenty-person dinner, especially if I'm not doing any matchmaking ahead of time. I'm wondering from a practical standpoint, as the host (and business owner), if guests would ultimately deem the evening "unsuccessful" if they left without making a potential romantic connection, regardless of whether every other element (great food, safe environment, inspiring conversation) is thoughtfully considered and orchestrated on their behalf.

Eventually, I have the idea to shift the event format from a sit-down dinner to a larger gathering for about one hundred people.

While an intimate dinner is a great way to learn a lot about someone quickly, the potential matchmaking element and the odds of compatibility seem daunting, so in opening the night up to more people, there's more potential for matches (there's probably a math word for this or, like, a marketing word? Something about *probability*).

I team up with a fancy hotel in Toronto, and we set a date for our first Single With Strangers, the week before Valentine's Day. I create cards for multiple rounds of small-group conversations that encourage people to talk about their interests, hobbies, backgrounds, and accomplishments, thinking of questions that would emulate what people talk about on first dates. We'll scramble the groups each time so people get to talk to lots of people throughout the night. I invite my friend Tychon Carter to cohost with me, bringing his charm and charisma to the evening. Tychon is a multihyphenate creative (and also a *Big Brother Canada* winner—cool!), and his work centers on inspiring vulnerable conversations between men—a great complement to the Dinner With Strangers mission. Women's tickets sell out in an hour and a half, with the men's getting claimed within a few days. We get dressed up and set out to see if we can get a room of one hundred singles to mix and mingle with openness and curiosity.

After guests arrive, Tychon and I get onstage and talk about the state of dating culture in Toronto, bantering about dating apps and ghosting and how a part of me dies anytime I've been on a dating app and someone asks me about my favorite color or answers, "Not much, how about you?" when I ask what they're up to that weekend (give me *something* to go off of, dude). I talk about how Dinner With Strangers started, and how quickly we can get to know each other when everyone is willing to open up and listen well and allow themselves to be surprised by each other. I invite them to take a different approach to dating tonight: gathering with lots of different people—even regardless of initial attraction—and asking thoughtful questions to see what they might learn about and from each other.

After I share the logistics of organizing into groups of six or so on their own—while planning for the event, we had a lot of back-and-forth on whether to assign groups for everyone, but that felt *unsexy* to me, like we were organizing a networking event—the room nervously chatters and begins to sort themselves. I do a lap, handing out the first round of question cards, before a group of three women call for my attention.

"We don't have men to join our group," they tell me, looking a little annoyed. "Can you find us men to talk with?" The room has settled into pockets of conversation, so I suggest that they divide and conquer, each joining a different group, rather than my disrupting the groups that have already formed and "pulling" men to join them. The women glance around the room and look back at me.

"Which groups are we supposed to join?" one asks. I offer, "The group beside you only has four people in it. Why don't you join them?" They look at the group—meaning: they survey the *men* in the group—and look back at me again. They don't move. I stare back at them. It occurs to me in real time that they don't just mean "Can you find us men to talk to?" but rather "Can you find us men *we're attracted to* that we can talk to?" I say again that the hope for the night is that people get to interact with all sorts of people, and they're welcome to join whichever group they'd like.

The night, overall, is a success, by which I mean people meet and talk and seem to have a good time. There's a different feel to the night, though, one of urgency. One of comparison, or at least strong assessment, of how someone might measure up to someone else, or what it might say about us if someone we're interested in reciprocates that interest or not. As if each person isn't just asking, "Who are you?" but, "Who are you, and are you interested in who I am, and what does *your* interest in *me* say about *me* as a person?"

I think of an event I hosted only two months earlier, which had the same format as Single With Strangers but wasn't a dating event, and I can decipher a distinct difference in people's ease with approaching each other, the way they interacted, and the increased atmosphere of comfort in the room. People were encouraged to approach each other and interact and were happy to do so. They were free to be fascinated by each other and could find common-alities and conversational chemistry without it *meaning anything.* The added element of simply calling something an *event for singles* is enough to shift the way people interact and what they're looking for from the evening. Instead of showing up and seeing what hap-pens, seeing whom they meet and connect with, and seeing how they feel about what ends up happening, they feel a pressure that a specific, elusive *something* is supposed to happen.

Dating events, and even online dating apps, serve a great purpose: They act as an intentional meeting place for singles in the same proximity to find each other, taking away a bit of the chance and randomness of meeting someone *in the wild.* They bring us all to the same location, a convenient and practical way of organizing ourselves to find people who are in the same scenario, potentially looking for the same thing—in this case, to find someone who is likewise single and available and hoping to find someone to date. But it's really no different from going to any networking event with the ideal outcome being that you make some strategic connections and get some fresh leads, or joining any club (be it running or knitting or reading or what have you) and hoping you find people who share not only the same interests as you but may also be *your type of people.*

There's an added vulnerability to a desired outcome at a dating event: to explicitly declare ourselves single and *looking*—"looking" meaning hoping that people won't just like us but will also potentially find us attractive, interesting, appealing, desirable… And we perceive and internalize it as rejection if that desired outcome doesn't happen—never mind all the variabilities that go into any given gathering: who's free that night, who heard about the event, who signed up for it or didn't. Maybe our *most compatible person ever* was tied up that evening, maybe in New York, maybe home with a cold—who's to know how the universe math works out on that equation?

I wonder if it's at all possible to go into any of these situations with as open a mind as people do at a "regular" Dinner With Strangers. How going into a situation with an attitude of *let's see what this night has in store for me* instead of *I hope the elusive person I'm picturing for myself shows up tonight* shifts our mindset and allows us to receive whatever new interactions, fresh perspectives, and potential connections—romantic and otherwise—might come our way.

I first learn about subconscious expectations being crushed with the advent of my first kiss, which was, admittedly, pretty lame. I'm fourteen, working at a summer camp and crushing on (and flirting with) an emo skater boy (who's also interested in rocket science because he contains multitudes) who's on the kitchen crew. We've spent a handful of evening campfires sitting close to each other, knees touching and the like, finding excuses to run into each other in the mess hall, spending afternoons down by the water, under a tree, sharing about our teenage angst, swapping music suggestions for our iPods.

One night before the camp-wide game of capture the flag (*I know, I know,* it's so cliché, but I swear these are the circumstances; what can I do about it?) I'm sitting with Skater Boy and three of his kitchen comrades on a bench by the lake. One minute the boys are talking about football and the next minute Skater Boy leans (leaps? lunges?) over and we are suddenly kissing—or at least, *our lips are touching*. I can hardly process what is happening. His friends are sitting *right there*. Never mind that he doesn't know this is my very first kiss in the history of my life, this is *our* first kiss, and he's just, what, going to make out with me on this bench while his friends talk about touchdowns and the merits of cheering for a specific team regardless of their national standing? Skater Boy has some things to learn about setting and timing, that's for certain.

I pull away quickly, deeply embarrassed by the scenario. Because of the other three people (*boys!!!!!!*) present, I can't even say *I don't know what I'm doing re: kissing, can you walk me through this* or *can we try that again later* or *maybe can you try that again when there aren't other people with us and also what were you thinking, did you think I'd LIKE that setup?!!!* and instead I do what any reasonably awkward teenager would do: I get up and pretty much run away. My ears are hot and I can hear my heartbeat reverberating in my skull.

I run to my cabin, where a gaggle of my cabinmates are getting ready for the night's activities, curling irons and straighteners lining the bathroom counter and living room floor, the smell of sizzled hair and beach-scented body spray wafting through the air. I tell them that Skater Boy kissed me—"But like, we weren't alone???"—and the group of girls immediately assembles to dissect and translate the significance of the whole situation: how long was the kiss and maybe he was nervous and maybe he just *really* wanted to kiss me, etc.

I wanted to be excited, but I confess, "I just thought my first kiss would be…different. Like a little more momentous, a little less by surprise," trying not to sound disappointed, still in a bit of shock that it happened at all, wondering if it even *counted* as a kiss.

Angela, a wise-beyond-her-years lifeguard, offers, "Maybe it feels extra disappointing because you were envisioning something specific without even realizing it. Like imagining a blue birthday cake with flowers on it, but not voicing that or even realizing your ideal cake would be blue with flowers on it until your friends bring out your actual cake, and it's pink or whatever. Maybe it even has multiple tiers and is even more elaborately decorated, but there's still this weird tinge of disappointment because it wasn't the way you were expecting it to be."

I think the metaphorical cake equivalent to my first kiss is one that is half-baked with gloopy icing on it, smeared on like an afterthought. And it's okay that I'm disappointed when that's the caliber of cake I'm handed, whether I'm envisioning a specific color and shape of cake or not. It's tough to accept that some people's first kisses are wholesome, or passionate, or straight out of a movie scene, when mine was not. Soon enough I will kiss someone on a boardwalk, gently and unhurried. I'll kiss at sunset, at midnight. I will be kissed in doorways and on back porches, in Ecuador and Paris and once when he comes after me on his bike when I've stormed off, steaming mad that he half-professes his feelings when he saw another guy talking to me at his brother's birthday but is still "too scared to do anything about it." That particular kiss is one for the history books. I'll know what it's like to swoon, to lean in, to melt, just like they say can happen. And quickly I'll learn that it's impossible to predict what kind of cake's going to show up before it does. Best not envision it. Just put the fork down when you encounter a bad one. The good stuff is on the way.

———

I meet Sasha on a dating app in the spring of 2024 and we go on a couple of dates, relating to each other's former evangelical backgrounds and our mutual love of Rainer Maria Rilke, quickly finding our own shorthand in talking, meandering around the city via the long, scenic route home to make the night last longer. He asks me a few times in a few different ways *what it is I'm looking for.* I'm secretly hung up on a particular emotionally unavailable, deeply avoidant muse (not my first, but please god, hopefully my last), but I can't bring THAT up on a date. I give some answer about being pretty focused on work right now but hoping for some Great Love if it found me.

After multiple attempts to get a straight answer out of me, Sasha says, "Jess, I really like you, and I really want to get to know you, and I don't think that's going to happen if we keep dating, so I'd rather be your friend." I realize after he says this (and after I first respond a bit defensively) that taking the pressure of "dating" off our getting to know each other somehow opens me up to be myself with him. After we stop dating, Sasha gets to meet the real me.

My friendship with Sasha ironically teaches me more about romantic relationships—or, more accurately, how *I* am in romantic relationships—all thanks to our not being in a romantic relationship with each other. I practice speaking up and speaking about how something makes me feel as the feelings arise. I let him know quickly when his indecisiveness and tendency to change his mind about how we should spend our afternoon are driving me *absolutely bonkers* instead of putting the pressure on myself to whiplash along with him and try to think of four new suggestions for every *new vibe* he thinks he wants to cultivate. We show up for each other on hard days, run errands on each other's behalf, chat on the phone without scheduling a call. I pull a muscle in my back in the summer and wonder if it's within our friendship creed to ask him to come hang out; I'm not so injured that I can't order myself takeout and hobble to the front door to get it, but it would be nice to have some company. Unprompted, he texts, "Hey bud! What are you up to tonight?" and I say, "I pulled my back actually. I'm pretty pathetic right now!" and he responds, "Oh no, that's awful! I'll come make you dinner! Any requests?" instead of the usual *well, let me know if you need anything,* which can make it so impossible to decide what counts as a need. We practice over and over many different ways to care for each other without needing to define our relationship, much to the confusion of our mothers.

I've learned to let who Sasha is in relation to me emerge on its own, rather than holding up a ledger in front of him, seeing if he meets the criteria for what I think I'm looking for in a partner and, if he doesn't meet it, moving on. In doing so, we've written our own kind of love story, the kind that finds us driving each other to early-morning ferries and quenching late-night ice cream cravings, debriefing our latest dates, and saying *I love you* freely and unabashedly when we hang up the phone and when we hug goodbye. We mean it with our whole hearts, just not in *that* way.

———

The fact that we mostly only celebrate romantic love, and mostly try to figure out if it's the *forever* kind of love or not, holds us back from embracing all the other love stories in our lives or imagining any other kind of meaningful connection between people other than a romantic storyline. I'm late for drinks with friends because I had a two-hour meeting with a brewery owner in town, and they immediately ask if there's something going on between us, not what kind of fun business collaboration we're dreaming up together. I post online a video from my (guy) friend's concert, and I get twenty DMs asking if this is *my new man*. When we first start dating, Andrew leaves from his first visit to Toronto, and my mom asks if she should be saving for a wedding instead of asking me how I feel about him. Cal and I never really dated per se, but we're simply real friends now; he makes me a custom bike rack at this woodworking shop, packs his bag with old-fashioneds sealed in mini mason jars for our day trip to Toronto Island (complete with orange twist), tells me the story about his brother in a hushed voice, listens while I ramble about my latest worry. Back when we weren't-really-dating-but-we-were-sort-of-something, I was hyperaware of how often I initiated our texts back and forth, being sure to not be *too much,* hoping to come off as *chill.* Now he is the honored recipient of any goofy raccoon video I come across on social media and I am unfazed if I send three or four in a row. We go to concerts, send links to great vintage coats, alert each other at any new discovery of an exceptional croissant.

Somewhere, a plate made out of oyster shells that were shucked by a chef hangs on the wall of his restaurant. The plate was made by a ceramicist who knows how to take one thing that used to be alive and turn it into something new with her own two hands. The chef, who is really a poet, tells me that Japan gifted thousands of oyster seeds to the U.S. to plant on the West Coast to mark the end of the trade embargo between the two countries in the 1940s. Decades later, after a tsunami devastates Japan's coast, the U.S. sends Japanese oyster seeds back to their home to repopulate its waters. The chef and I are made of the same things and speak the same language and never manage to say what we actually mean. Sometimes the things that show up as gifts don't make sense until they're cast out to sea. If none of that is a love story, it's at least a poem that you can feel in your teeth.

———

We've been fed one kind of love story: one about romantic love whose strength is measured by its duration and starts a certain way. One that we should all be looking for and holding out for and should recognize immediately when it arrives. But we need to hear more love stories, and not just about the beginning of a relationship, when everything seems shiny and hopeful and easy. We need love stories about romantic love, long-worn and still going, but also about the friends who've known each other since childhood, and friends who found each other late in life. When we remember and remind each other that so many forms of love exist, we find undeniable proof that love is endlessly expansive, showing up in different ways, meeting our multifaceted needs and wants and desires in different quantities in each relationship, no one-size-fits-all, no one single love to eclipse the rest.

We need to hear more love stories about the things new parents laugh about at 4 a.m. while passing a screaming baby back and forth, no sleep for any of them.

We need love stories about brothers. And men in general, asking each other about their feelings.

We need love stories about all the things left on friends' porches. And all the love stories about people who wave at each other on the street.

We need more love stories about women choosing themselves, loving themselves, prioritizing rest and peace and opting out without explanation.

We need to hear more love stories about people who have been together for thirteen years, still bringing each other a glass of water unprompted. And the things they continue to argue about—either silly and small or the argument that turns the room into lava but they keep returning to it, and to each other, as if to ask *will you still meet me?*

We need love stories about people who met at the wrong time.

And the right time. We need to hear more love stories about love that felt more like a quiet afternoon rather than fireworks exploding in the sky. We need more love stories that start with *first I messed everything up and then…* We need to hear more love stories about not getting most of it right.

We need to hear more love stories about someone walking into a tiny wine bar in a different city on a random night in March and meeting someone who will turn out to be their favorite person to dream with, and argue with, and say everything except how either of them actually feels with, who happened to be wearing a purple corduroy shirt the day they met, which is only relevant in the way that every single detail feels relevant in a love story. We need to hear every love story about anyone who's changed someone's life once they realized that the other person existed, regardless of how far into the depths they were able to go together, or for how long, or what it looked like to the outside world, or what name they gave it.

We need more love stories about all the people we loved and never told, loved and couldn't be with, loved and let go, loved and still had to leave.

We need more love stories about looking ourselves in the mirror, with all our self-neglect and self-abandonment and self-loathing. We need to realize that if we find something gentle to say to ourselves in this moment, then this is a love story too.

14

The Table Where We Meet

Meeting Requires Reverence for Each Other

I grew up in a non-yelling household, which is not to say there wasn't any tension. Collectively, we were not quick (or skilled) at expressing displeasure or disappointment, or stating our needs, desires, and boundaries. Keeping the peace, treating each other *nicely*, reacting *well*, upholding docile conduct and a calm demeanor: These were highly valued attributes, passed down through generations of pacifists and codependents with maladaptive tools for communication and conflict resolution.

I had powerful doses of internalized religious guilt and shame layered in there as well; to admit wrongdoing or to act out in anger meant that I'd committed a sin, making me *sinful*, making me *bad*. I'd avoid admitting fault, hiding my mishaps and spinning narratives to avoid being found out for what I was (which was: a human).

I've worked very hard at conflict resolution; it took me a long time to not receive the slightest sliver of constructive feedback as an attack on my character or a deep and wholehearted rejection of self. Until my mid-twenties, I dealt with almost all conflict with the effective and constructive slogan of *Retreat and Withdraw!* Better to slip away into myself at the first sign of danger, build a massive fortress, and not let anyone in.

I've had to learn how to receive people's feedback or invitations to have difficult conversations as an act of deep love (when delivered in a loving way). That someone saying "This thing hurt my feelings—can we talk about it?" doesn't translate to "Hey, not sure if you noticed, but you are a terrible person! Irrevocably flawed, in fact! And undeserving of any kind of closeness with anyone in your life ever!" This has come with time and effort and exposure therapy to constructive conflict with loving, patient friends, family, and partners who have held my hand gently, taught me how to speak up, and demonstrated how to delicately navigate difficult conversations. It means that someone cares enough, and trusts enough, to knead out the knots together. It means that the investment of discomfort is worth the effort. It means they believe that we can repair, learn, and grow from this.

And when it comes to *disagreeing* on something—with people I know and people I love, as well as strangers on the internet and beyond—I for the most part have a long way to go in regard to staying calm and centered, and thus able to stay in the conversation. Usually, my ears get hot and I get a lump in my throat and I get upset really quickly. I shut down, I take it all personally, I have to remind myself to *not* take everything so personally. With friends who have vastly different beliefs than mine, the best I've been able to do is draw a boundary and say, *"Because I love you, we can't talk about this."* This approach *keeps the peace*—as in, keeps things civil, keeps things in check, keeps things orderly—but it doesn't get us anywhere new. It doesn't allow us to embark anywhere together. It doesn't invite us to perhaps identify our own ignorance, biases, or defensiveness. It doesn't allow for us to find the through-thread of why someone has taken the stance they have, to get curious about the roots of a belief, or what a belief might be protecting about our identity or our understanding of the world and our place within it.

———

I don't think we societally are doing a great job at talking things through in a constructive way, or even *initiating* difficult conversations where we share how we feel and actually say what we mean (hi, have you ever seen a movie? Miscommunication is like the premise of All the Movies of All Time, mostly). This is made worse by social media becoming our main watering hole and gathering place for news and sappy discourse on what to think about what's going on in the world. For the most part, we're not actually talking *with* each other.

It goes like this: I follow accounts (which is to say, people) who share things I like (maybe: home decor, maybe: sports, maybe: makeup tips, maybe: poetry, maybe: adorable dogs who can juggle) and who mostly say things I mostly agree with. I then repost their content (maybe: artistic pictures of people holding massive bouquets of flowers, maybe: quippy sound-bite-like info slides or punchy quotes or mic-drop video clips of people saying something really clearly to the point), which shares their post with my audience (which is to say, people) of most likely more or less similar-thinking people with similar interests. This creates an echo chamber of likes and shares and saves, and comments like *totally agree* and *exactly this* and many, many fire emojis. If someone slips through who disagrees with this quippy-pithy-mic-drop post of mine, it is rare for them to engage in discourse of any kind, and if they, heaven forbid, voice their disapproval or varied opinion from mine, it's easy to write them off as *just not my kind of people* and keep it moving along.

The algorithm feeds us what we've trained it to feed us, the intention being to keep our attention. Stay on the app. See more content you like, stay engaged, stay longer. Oh, you liked this post about funky vintage sneakers? Here are forty other accounts that feature funky vintage sneakers; maybe you'd like to look at each of them and maybe eventually buy something. Oh, you like bespoke DIY furniture glow-ups? Here's more of that. Oh, you accidentally clicked on a video of a very giant pimple? You will now be unable to escape these so-gross-but-you-can't-look-away zit-popping montages; you're welcome. So by nature, media platforms have become domains of aligned social, political, and philosophical views too; we see a post that resonates with us, we like it or save it or even repost it, and then we are sent more content in the same vein, while content that contradicts what we've told the algorithm we enjoy and believe is kept out.

The upside to this is that we are introduced to creatives and artists who move and inspire us—businesses, makers, and doers who are offering something we love, and educators, advocates, organizations, and activists with brilliant information and incredible resources. Let's also not forget that the success of my work is directly tied to The Powers of the Internet, helping tenderhearted feelers find their way to my swirling mind displayed on the screen.

The spiraling road of the algorithm also creates chasms between the things we are interested in and the things we're not interested in, the things we like and the things we don't like, the things we agree with and the things we don't agree with. It places us in our silos of thought. And because of its design—us with our own individual platforms where we can say and post whatever we want; us with our little screens in our hands, staring at words that inspire and ignite us, or otherwise words that enrage us and entice us to clap back—we get to work making a quick comment that is more rewarded for being biting or provoking than for being patient, caring, and inquisitive. We do so without the feedback of seeing the person on the other side of their little screen and how our words land on them. It is largely not designed for nuanced discourse or healthy discussion from varied or opposing views, and yet social media has largely become the place where we hash out our differences and disagreements. We post mic-drop rebuttals and tell each other why we're wrong. We're quick to announce that we're unfollowing someone for something they said or an organization they support that doesn't align with our own views and values.

We forget that life doesn't happen on social media; it can feel like we're caught up with each other's lives because we see our friend's carousel of their camping trip or our uncle's post about his new job or our coworker's video montage of their wedding anniversary. It's beautiful that we get these glimpses and updates, especially for loved ones who live far away, but it's not a replacement for actual connection with each other in the *real world*, or even the full picture of how anyone is actually doing. How often have we posted our own highlight reels of trips, dinners, Friday nights out, and omitted the argument in the car on the way there, the slight or severe annoyances that happen in between the pictures, the feelings, frustrations, and fears we're carrying at any given time that may or may not be related at all to whatever we're posting about? In a similar vein, we form conclusions about each other's views, maybe even distancing ourselves from someone after seeing something they post (if a differing opinion even makes its way into our feed in the first place), instead of reaching out to have a conversation about how their post made us feel.

We're becoming increasingly unversed in engaging with each other in constructive ways, and the way we use these platforms as a replacement for in-person connection as well as the way they're designed to affirm and enforce our tastes, preferences, and ideologies siphons us further away from each other. We stick to our inner circles, we follow and then unfollow people flippantly, we move through most public spaces as if we're in our own bubbles, rarely intersecting with others in attendance—I always consider this when I'm at a concert, wondering where I land on the spectrum of fandom in relation to the five thousand other people in the arena, how long they've been listening to his particular band, and what else we might all have in common other than our taste in music. We keep to ourselves even within these commonalities, and we use differences and disagreements as ways to further separate ourselves from each other.

Dinner With Strangers, in its simplest form, is a cultural revolution just by the act of people congregating without vetting if anyone is like-minded or has similar interests or comes from the same place. We sit next to and across from people we've never met and partake in welcoming each other with curiosity, getting a peek into someone's life, experience, and perspective for a night. There is hardly any desired outcome beyond inviting people to witness each other; no one is required to change anyone's mind or have their own mind changed. No one is required to like anyone or agree with anyone or stay in touch with anyone. People can very well come for dinner, listen and observe and talk a bit, and then fade into the night, never to see each other again.

I believe in the necessity to meet each other in our differences. To find a way to see each other from across the divide. To try to map how we each got to the conclusions we've reached and the lenses through which we perceive the world and ourselves within it. How might we make our neighborhoods, communities, and societies more robust in safety and respect for one another? There is a proverbial table at which this process takes place, and in order to meet each other at the table, we must consider what *conditions* are necessary for any sort of sharing, or discourse, or even conflict to take place in a safe, supportive, constructive way. And we need to examine what the components are that prevent us from being able to pull out a chair and sit down; meeting each other isn't mandatory, and everyone is within their right to opt out of gathering here, especially when a baseline of respect and security isn't established. And yet by sequestering ourselves only with those who think like us and see the world as we do, the trench continues to splinter even deeper. How do we possibly proceed? How can we not try to find a way?

The conditions I'm talking about go so far beyond *niceness* or *civility*, which would include conditions like *we shouldn't yell at each other* or *one person speaks at a time*. These are good ground rules of how to conduct ourselves and treat each other in any conversation, tense or otherwise (baseline respect: we love to see it), but the presence of this type of conduct doesn't necessarily mean we are doing a good job at *hearing* each other or *taking care of* each other.

This is all well and good when we are talking about the hippie and the investment banker having dinner for the night. The stay-at-home parent and the intentionally childless mid-thirties person pass the potatoes between them with ease, getting an intriguing, brief peek into a life not chosen. But what are we to do when it feels like someone's beliefs are in direct opposition with our very being? What are we to do when we know that recognizing ourselves in each other's stories is a powerful catalyst for change and revelation, but sharing our stories with someone who's vehemently against our lifestyle / worldview / political party / approach to parenting / sexual orientation / entire country where we're from feels risky—even dangerous? Is it even possible to proceed when *agree to disagree* isn't remotely enough?

This isn't about everybody *getting along*. This is about learning how to greet each other's stories with an incredible amount of honor and reverence. This is about valuing each person's experience above our set of beliefs about what is the "right" way to live a life. This is about creating completely new terms with which we interact in order to try to understand each other, each story and insight acting as a clue to these mysteries: What is it like to be you? What are all the elements and histories and contexts that have shaped the way you see the world and the way you move through it? What have you experienced that informs what you value and prioritize? What feels most fragile? What, or who, do you want to protect the most? What causes do you most care about, and why are those important to you?

———

I'm hosting our second Dinner With Strangers since officially launching as a business—it's my second dinner with twenty-three guests, and maybe my fifth dinner ever where I've charged for tickets. My impostor syndrome is blaring: People are paying for this experience and I'm still finding my footing with what the heck this project is, how to feed all these people, how to make the business side of it remotely profitable, and how to get a handle on what I'm doing so that energetically it's sustainable to run multiple times a month if I decide to do that.

Guests ascend on October 12, 2023, which is a few days after Canadian Thanksgiving; our theme is "How Do You Feel About Gratitude?" I have three questions prepared for the group, starting with "What is a decision you're glad you made?" and then "What is something you like about yourself?" We're halfway through the second question, and while I love forcing people to say nice things about themselves, the conversation is missing some grit, some depth, some *oomph*. On the fly, I decide to add in, "What is something you're finding it difficult to be grateful for right now?"

People lean into the question, sharing about struggling to feel grateful for the independence of being single, for jobs they are lucky to have and don't absolutely love, for the kids they love who drive them to their last nerve of sanity, for seasons that test patience, and we nod along with each other: *Yes, I know that feeling. I understand.*

Next it's Joy's turn to share.

Joy shares that her family lives in Israel, and her sister's backyard was bombed five days ago. The energy in the room immediately shifts; we all know we have entered new ground. She shares, "Given the question, am I grateful that they are all 'intact'? Yes, I am grateful for that. Should 'intact' be the ultimate goal? No. We are terrified. Everyone is heartbroken."

A few people later, Oksana shares that she is from Ukraine, with many family members currently living in the middle of a war zone. She speaks to Joy directly, understanding the many complicated emotions of being the person who is in Canada while loved ones are in a place where bombs are being dropped in their backyards. Oksana continues, "I would be remiss if I didn't say how terrified I am on behalf of the people of Palestine for the retaliation to come as a result of Hamas's attack on the seventh. I think innumerable civilians will pay the price."

The table falls into a palpable silence; the simple mention of specific countries is loaded with connotation and subtext of what each place might *mean* to any of us, or *where we might stand*—on a specific side of a line, for instance. A line that might look like a border. A border that might delineate where our empathy begins and ends (here are these people who are afraid on behalf of the people they love) and the context that we choose to consider, disregard, or cling to (here are these people, from *these* places, which hold all sorts of meanings—conclusions, assumptions—about who they are and what they believe and who is important to them and what they think is right and wrong and what they might think is "justified" violence).

Because I'm so green in my facilitation skills, and still incredibly conflict-averse (meaning: discomfort-of-any-kind averse), I pull a bit of a rookie move: I fuddle through something about *how awful it all is*—speaking in generalities instead of acknowledging the shift in the room and the uncharted territory in which we find ourselves. I say something about my desire for peace and safety, maybe sounding a bit like a Miss America contestant saying all the right buzzwords while saying not-quite-anything. I ramble through paraphrasing a few lines from a poem by Padraig Ó Tuama, a writer and longtime conflict resolution facilitator at Corrymeela, a center for peace and reconciliation in Northern Ireland. In "The Pedagogy of Conflict," Ó Tuama says that the only way to count lives lost in conflict is like this: "one life / one life / one life… because each time / is the first time / that that life has been taken."[1]

Ó Tuama grew up during the Troubles in Ireland, which devastated nations, and land that was argued over, and generations of people, by launching bombs and hatred at each other. He often talks about the painful, slow, necessary work of somehow finding a way to meet each other, because the alternative is continual destruction. Perpetual annihilation. And I do believe in the moral necessity of ceasing fire, in all directions; we don't need to be an expert in any country's political history to insist that violence begets more violence, that literal bombs create philosophical chasms that prevent us from seeing ourselves in each other. And yet using force and violence is our decided-upon currency of retaliation, as if retaliation makes anything right.

But I use Padraig's poem to try to rescue the room from

---

1 Padraig Ó Tuama, *Sorry for Your Troubles* (Dublin: Canterbury Press Norwich, 2013).

discomfort, moving us on to the next question to shift the energy of the room, missing a potentially sacred moment by not addressing the power, and maybe the pain and difficulty, in the fact that we were all somehow here together, and what might we make of its meaning?

In hindsight, I could've said something like, "Wow, this is as real as it gets, here at the intersection of each of our stories, and the places we're from, and how they're related to each other, and the tension that exists in these realities. And how beautiful that we might meet each other as humans, humans who care about the people we love, and who hope for safety, and hopefully are dreaming of a better way forward for all of us." Perhaps this would've opened the conversation up for a conversation about times we've opted for deescalation instead of retaliation. Instead of naming the moment, calling out the palpable tension in the air, I am eager to get to sturdier ground together.

Here at the table, there is a sister who is afraid for her family's safety. There is a woman to her right who sees the writing on the wall for the atrocities that are to come. To my immediate left is a woman whose partner is from Palestine, who teaches her how to make taboon bread that they dip in mansaf on Fridays. And these are not three people whose perspectives, stories, and motivations are separate from each other; these are three people whose perspectives, stories, and motivations are inextricably woven together, like the weave of the softly spun gauze that we hold against a gaping wound.

Each of them is advocating for someone's liberation, safety, and freedom. And to advocate for anyone's liberation, safety, and freedom is to insist on those things for all; if our definition of liberation is dependent on the suppression (or, god help us, the annihilation) of a people, that is not liberation at all. We can only go somewhere together—*get* somewhere together—if we're able to recognize that liberation, safety, and freedom are inherently deserved by *everyone*, and it is up to us to ardently protect each other, to reflect on the ways we might be complicit in causing harm—inadvertently or accidentally or intentionally or otherwise.

———

The world, in so many ways, feels insurmountably divided. I believe in the necessity of diminishing that division by finding a way to see each other, even in our difficult and flawed humanness. I believe in the radical, transformative power of sharing our stories with each other. I believe that centering our humanity at the heart of any conversation quiets many of the seemingly complex issues of our time. I believe we can find a lot of empathy for each other when we remember that every single person is made up of the histories and contexts and nuances of the places they're from and what the people they love have endured. We have all survived something, many things, in fact, which have shaped how we see the world, how we express ourselves, what we care about, and what specific things break our hearts.

And still we divide and define ourselves in so many ways as *us* and *them*.

It's summer 2024. I'm on vacation with my family in Union, Washington, a tiny town on the Olympic Peninsula. My dad and I drive five minutes from our cabin to pick up some pizzas, and as we pull into the parking lot, there is a massive truck parked out front, tires the size of tanks, the bed of the truck nearly clearing my forehead. It's covered in bumper stickers: slogans declaring who specifically is not welcome in the great country of the United States of America. Proclamations of ill will toward certain politicians. At least eight different stickers claim that tragedies in the country are conspiracies—*fake news,* if you will. Sprawling American flags flank each side of the cabin, cozied up beside flags with another certain politician's campaign flag of equal size. I realize I feel two feet tall, frozen but alert to every subtle movement around me, as if I'm prey and a predator is lurking. According to the decrees of the bumper stickers, I know that I could pass as someone "acceptable" to be here. My fear turns to disgust and fury.

We walk into the pizza place with the bell on the door welcoming us, the TV on the wall glowing with the Mariners game. Just as I wonder to myself if we'll be able to tell who the truck belongs to, I notice the man in front of us: mountainous in his six-foot-four stature and wearing a foam neck brace. He's wearing a hat, T-shirt, and basketball shorts all boasting the name or various catchphrases of the politician broadcast on the truck outside. I've never been much of a merch girlie myself, but I guess it's (almost) cute that he's gone all-in on his number one guy. A young boy appears from the bathroom and joins the merch-clad giant. He softly puts his mitt of a hand on the boy's head and lightly tousles his hair. The man realizes we're standing behind him and moves over slightly, saying, "You guys go ahead. We've already ordered."

My dad (who used to tousle *my* hair when we were standing in various lines on various vacations until one day I started to care that it would totally mess up my hairstyle) and I get back in his stickerless white Subaru. I relay my internal experience of the last five minutes: intimidation, revulsion, anger, judgment, frustration, scorn. I question, "Is that the intention, do you think? Not just broadcasting an endorsement for a politician or party, but sending a message? Making sure we *feel it*? He must realize how discriminatory so many of those stickers are. How insulting. Imagine taking pleasure in that?"

This man has made it known what he believes and where he stands, and who he believes is welcome (and not welcome) near him. It's difficult for me to imagine a world where I would feel comfortable making neighborly talk while standing in line for our pizza order, or mustering anything kind to say for that matter. Somehow imagining myself extending warmth to this man feels like a betrayal of the people he so explicitly outlines as abhorrent, invalid, and unworthy. The notion of coexisting as a diverse people with an eclectic array of worldviews and beliefs falls apart pretty quickly when those beliefs are discriminatory, harmful, and blatantly deny people basic human rights. Part of me feels compelled to yell in his face, declaring my own disapproval, speaking on behalf of those he's verbally slandered. I'm aware this will change nothing or, worse, it will wedge him even more firmly in his outlook. I wonder how much of this kind of reasoning is a cop-out from my speaking up against this kind of hate.

I wrestle with acknowledging the double standard of my desire to *change his mind* and wondering if there's anything I could do that might get through to him; if the tables were flipped, and he was searching for some way to convince me to change my stance on the ideologies we're clearly divided on, I'd say, "*As if! Good luck with THAT!*" We both feel equally justified and unwavering in our beliefs, and yet in my highest self, I implore the other versions of me to consider what kind of invitation to the proverbial table I might find within myself to extend to him.

The only ground we may be able to gain together might be to seek and find some humanity within each other, which can be reached only with mutual curiosity—meaning that a condition of this meeting place would require that he also be open to finding some humanity within me. My highest self would recommend not starting an inquiry with "Hey, man, have you considered how *hateful* you are?!" I can't get into listing all the ways I find his truck and its messages deeply offensive if I'm not willing to understand what's shaped his worldview. How did he end up living in this part of the state? What does he love about it? Who are the people most important to him? What does he fear on their behalf? What causes are important to him? Who in his opinion is making a positive difference? What do people often get wrong about him? What does he wish he could change?

Maybe this is less about considering how I could've engaged that specific man on that specific day and more about how my own personal, metaphorical truck of slogans and stickers might be preventing people from even attempting to open a dialogue with me, or keeping people from wanting to get close to me. Are there beliefs or behaviors that I wear like a provocation? Are there things I do or say that act like a giant "keep out" sign? What, generally, am I signaling and broadcasting through my actions? Who am I leaving out? Who else can I include? In what ways can I make the spaces I host safer, inclusive, and expansive?

If we concern ourselves with dismantling our own self-constructed barriers to connection, we're actively contributing a path to the table where we can all gather. We can only control the space that we choose to make for each other, which I hope includes enough elbow room for us to reach for what we need, and also a close enough proximity to each other that we can hear every word that anyone offers to the conversation.

I picture the table where we meet to be constructed out of our collective efforts and contributions: mismatched chairs and folding tables from our garages brought out to the street, all our different tablecloths creating a tapestry of our favorite colors and patterns, our different styles and aesthetics coming together to prepare the place where we gather. It is joyfully messy and imperfect, but what we offer we offer in earnest. We make a chorus from the sound of our voices. We make a potluck out of what we have—the food that we bring from our cupboards, the failures that have made us soft and humble, the turning points that have altered the direction of our lives. We hold heavy dishes for our neighbors as they fill their own plates. The dance that often happens over dinner works best when we take care to fill each other's glasses and make room for more seats at the table, more space for the stories that reveal something about our lives. Get the good glasses out for the street party. I want to know the story about how you came to be.

15

Tend to Your Porch

Take Care of What You Can

Here's something that embarrasses me about my current living situation (other than being a thirty-four-year-old who moved back in with roommates, which was supposed to be temporary and has somehow meandered into a multiyear stay and often feels like I'm an old has-been who can't get her financial shit together, so I'm imposing on these very cool mid- to late-twenties roommates who are just getting started with their lives[1]): This house, from the outside, is hideous—namely, but not exclusively, because of its

---

1 And then I have to remind myself that I'm a full-time working artist who also launched a business with high overhead all by myself without any funding, and baby, that takes time and energy and cold, hard cash and a whole lot of sacrifice, and having cheap rent in the west end of this beautiful city is nothing to be embarrassed of and my nineteen-year-old self would be absolutely stoked to find out that I found a way to make a living as an artist.

gross *carpeted* front porch. It is an objectively ugly threshold, with scratchy industrial-fiber fabric, made worse by an additional raised stretch of carpet (a solution to cover up what was worn down on the original) that runs from the front door all the way to the two steps down to the sidewalk.

The porch itself has bikes locked to the white faux-aluminum railings. A crooked, dented yellow snow shovel is resting against the pillar. A bin of salt that looks like a cat litter container should at least be put away when not in use for the winter months but instead stays there year-round. The organics bin for the house blocks a clear path to the door. The main-floor tenants' rejected treadmill is placed against the banister. A broom I can only assume came from the dollar store and that is definitely intended for indoor, noncarpet use is leaning next to the mailbox beside the doorbell (which doesn't actually ring).

It would be generous to say the house is *lacking curb appeal*. One of my roommates affectionately calls our house Garbage Palace. If a friend is coming over or meeting me at my house, I am quick to let them know I have the ugliest porch in the city, making sure they know that *I* know it's bad. Making sure they know that I'd never choose to have a porch that looks like this *if it were all up to me*. Making sure to distance myself from what the porch might *say about me*, my aesthetic, and all the status stuff that comes with the things we have and the places we live and the way we present ourselves to the world.

Because the front porch is carpeted, it clings to all debris that flies onto it: Dried leaves are crushed and nestled into the charcoal weave. Twigs and sticks have collected everywhere. All sorts of foliage is scattered about. The dollar store indoor broom is laughably ineffective in making a dent in the mess, so the tenants of all three apartments within this house have just allowed it to get to a state of near disrepair. Maybe, like me, everyone else thinks it's *not really their problem.* Maybe, like me, they've thought *it's too far gone to make a difference.* Maybe, like me, they've *left it to someone else* to put some work into cleaning the place up. Maybe, like me, they've thought this living situation is *temporary,* it's not actually *mine,* so why put any effort or, heaven forbid, *care* into it?

This morning as I get back from the gym, I unlock the front door and stare at the inner hallway that leads to the main-floor apartment and our upper three-bedroom-one-bathroom-no-dishwasher-but-great-windows-and-real-hardwood-and-hundred-year-old-crown-molding Girl Lair. The inner hallway is lined with shoes and boots and dog leashes that belong to five humans and one chatty husky. I decide that the floor of the hallway has gotten bad enough after a week of springtime rain: I will make it my problem to give it a quick sweep and thus feel good about myself for Doing the Bare Minimum to become the backbone of this household.

As I pick up the broom, I see a significant pile of dirt at its base from whoever had swept before me—nice of them to tidy up, funny that they didn't go as far as actually finishing the job and discarding the dust and dirt. The dented dustpan is *right there,* after all. I get the dustpan and sweep it all up and then decide to chip away a bit at the leaves and debris stuck in the carpet outside.

Initially I was going to just give it a quick once-over, but as I move things around, I realize the sweeping is actually making a bit of a difference to the appearance of the porch. I move the salt bin away from the front door and place it beside the rejected treadmill. I sweep around the bikes and get at the leaves that have collected in the doorjamb.

I find that the best technique for sweeping is to brush as softly as possible in order to get anything to move; the bristle of the carpet is too strong for the wimpy supposed-to-be-for-the-kitchen broom. By presenting its stubbornness, it requires me to respond with gentleness. The harsher the element, the more ease I have to bring. Slowly and patiently, the porch is swept.

My fifteen minutes of mild effort yield okay-ish results (it is still, after all, a carpeted porch with a bunch of junk on it). And it makes me think about ownership, as in the things I claim to be my responsibility, as in the things I put my name behind, the things I make my problem (and my solution). I didn't intend to live in this apartment past spring, and I've been using the excuse that it isn't my place (or responsibility) to make any change or make any effort toward improving the space. Some things feel so ugly—that is, so beyond hope—that we avoid even attempting to contribute to making them better for ourselves and for the people around us.

———

I think we use the same sentiments I use for my porch as justifications for not creating the kinds of communities we want to be a part of, and not creating the kind of world we want. At Dinner With Strangers, people often express their frustration around finding community and connection in their cities. People are cold, distant, and flaky, and it's discouraging to feel like nobody cares.

We are made to feel like our contributions don't matter or won't make a difference. We forget that every contribution toward making this world a better place counts, adds up, and contributes to something better. We're waiting for someone else to pick up the broom. We often worry more about who initiated the not-caring than about being the one to start caring and putting in some effort. We worry that we will be the only one working hard and start tallying efforts instead of rolling up our sleeves to do what we can. We fall victim to that weird high school attitude of thinking it's cool to think everything is lame instead of opting into something that might be fun even if it looks cheesy at first glance.

Apathy is an incredibly useful tool: It's way more comfortable and convenient than admitting disappointment, than facing the fact that we're not where we want to be or, deeper than that, that maybe we are incredibly heartbroken or incredibly lonely or incredibly let down by something or someone. It's easier to avert our eyes than to look at the unsightly thing. It's easier to throw our hands up and say *what can we really do about it* or to point fingers or to say that something else other than us is really the REAL problem. The sinister Powers That Be bank on our apathy, too, that we will doomscroll the tragedies and mess and trauma and toxicity that feel so big and so awful and so beyond our control to the point of checking out and shutting down and averting our eyes to leave them to their dirty chess game of doing what they want.

It's easier to find ways in which we're exempt from responsibility than to admit the ways we're complicit in the issue at hand. It takes a lot of humility to examine our efforts and contributions and admit to the ways we've closed ourselves off from others and the ways we've added to the mess. It's easy—valid even (oooh and validity feels *so nice*)—to say that I was the last to move into this house and I don't want to step on anyone's toes by moving things around. Why should I be the one to create a new way of doing things or put in the time to clean up after what doesn't even feel like my mess? (How long has this crappy broom been here?! It's not *my* rejected treadmill to deal with! It's not *my* chatty husky that sheds like crazy!) But even if we're not the main culprit, we all play a part in the care and keeping of this house.

———

Someone at Dinner With Strangers shares that they're considering moving out of the city. "It's *changed*, you know," she says. "People are rude and impatient, people don't move out of the way on the sidewalk, it's loud and expensive and the art isn't the same and transit's not the same and there's no reason to stay anymore." This sentiment about Toronto has been floating around a lot since the beginning of the pandemic, and of course any city is always a living, breathing organism that is shaped by the people who live there (and this is to say nothing of the larger conversation about having livable, affordable cities so the people who shape it from all walks of life can remain living there). I've heard a similar sentiment in workplaces, at gyms and yoga studios, at restaurants and bars, and even in high school: "The culture sucks, everyone is closed off and rude, I don't like it here." We let our disappointment turn to cynicism and we separate ourselves, pull away, and disassociate from the things that feel salvageable and beautiful and worth cherishing in the name of not examining what's in our control to make a difference.

When I moved to San Francisco, I was thrilled to discover a new city and make it my own. Ever since I was a teenager, I always envisioned being a *California* girl—attributing all sorts of meaning to *what it would say about me* that I lived there, fully ready to leap into the stereotype of a chill, casual, green-juice-sipping, weekend-hiking, oyster-slurping West Coaster (never mind that these are generally attributed to people in LA; the rest of the world kind of doesn't know that). Quickly I discovered that people loved to hate San Francisco; many expats in the office would talk about how their home cities in their home states had better food and better work-life balance, cooler nightlife with better (cheaper!) cocktails and better music venues. People lamented the expensive rent and the rampant drug use in the Tenderloin and *all the people sleeping on the sidewalk who you have to step over on your way to work in the Financial District.* As if the people sleeping on the sidewalk are the problem, not the lack of resources in place to help them. I wanted to know what was worth salvaging, worth staying for, why here was a great place to build a life. I didn't want to conclude that the city was beyond hope.

This isn't to say that we must deny and avoid and reject criticism. In fact, I think the more we love a place, the more we should be checking the foundation for cracks and the beams for their integrity and the walls for any early signs of decay—not so we can flee at the earliest signs of decline but so we can respond with heartfelt action, care, and repair. I think often of James Baldwin's words in *Notes of a Native Son*[2]: "I love America more than any other country in the world and, exactly for this reason, I insist on the right to criticize her perpetually." No "house"—which is to say no community, no nation, no political party, no leader, no place that we gather—is above the investment of our criticism and reflection.

———

We live here. This is our planet and our country and our neighborhood and our home. And we are also visitors, here for a brief while. It's always harder to care than it is to wash our hands of taking initiative and ownership. Caring takes immense effort and searing optimism, which stings at the edges and feels fraught and small most of the time, like sweeping a hopelessly ugly carpeted porch with a dollar store broom.

It feels like I can barely do anything most of the time: I can't rip up the carpet and instead build a sturdy landing place. I can't

———

2 James Baldwin, *Notes of a Native Son* (Boston: Beacon Press, 1955).

change the structure or the orangey-dusty stone walls (we don't have time to get into the creepy plaque of St. Joseph on the front porch under the doorbell either) or the weird marble-facade countertops in the kitchen. But I can tend to the porch. I can sweep the leaves. I can stack my shoes with care, line up everyone else's in tidy rows. I can tread quietly through the hallway when I get home late.

I can do what I am able to do despite its inadequacies and finish my day knowing I did something to make this place a softer place to land.

16

We Don't Have to Do Any of This, but Maybe We Should Anyway
Take It Upon Yourself to Shift the Culture

I've made my travel itinerary to Las Vegas for my friend's wedding a bit more punishing than it maybe needed to be; sometimes the price jump between a layover (or two) and no layovers and between a 6 a.m. flight and a literally-any-other-time-to-take-a-flight flight is just too drastic to justify. So here I am, arriving at Toronto Pearson Airport at 3:47 a.m. without going to bed at all, thirteen minutes before the international customs and TSA even open, lining up with my fellow travelers, meaning I am in line with a bunch of people who are also en route to Las Vegas, meaning there are three identifiable groups of bachelor parties, adorned in their matching visors and beaded necklaces and T-shirts with comically unflattering pictures of their respective soon-to-be-groom bros cropped on the chest, clapping in sync as other dudes enter through the automatic doors one by one, arms outstretched, finger pistols to the sky, most of them sporting sunglasses to make the fluorescent lights more palatable at this hour, and all this coming to an absolute crescendo when one man of the hour, Brad, stumbles in with an extra-large coffee clutched in his hand—I know his name is Brad because chants of "BRAD! BRAD! BRAD!" commence immediately with overwhelming frat boy energy upon his arrival (of course his name has to be Brad; how could it have been any other name?).

The security gates open promptly at 4 a.m. and we shuffle with our roller suitcases and neck pillows[1] through the ropes that corral us in the direction we need to go. We are greeted by *the* cheeriest TSA agent I've ever come across. Shane (of course his name is Shane; how could it have been any other name?) is friendly and jovial and cracking jokes, his booming voice filling up the hangar-like room we find ourselves in, most of us bleary-eyed and caffeine-less. He gives us the efficiency and safety rundowns with carefully practiced puns about removing shoes and belts and putting our things neatly in the bins provided. He jokes that he will take our electronics and play Candy Crush Saga all day if we leave them behind, *so we'd better not!* He shakes hands with the grooms (Brad and his compatriots), razzes them a bit, says *happy wife, happy life!*

---

1 I make a note to consider once again the benefits of buying a neck pillow even though I've maintained a judgment that they look tacky and are annoying to carry around; as a complete aside, can someone take it upon themselves to *disrupt the neck pillow industry* and make unobnoxious neck pillows that actually travel well?

about eight times in a four-minute period. He asks those who have already had coffee to raise their hands, and those who need a coffee raise their hands next, points out people in the line who look like celebrities and asks for autographs (okay, that guy might have *actually* been a well-known football coach from the NFL; who am I to know?).

Shane is a one-man show, succeeding in making a room full of groggy, sleep-deprived travelers smile and giggle and shake their heads in amusement (even if it was also met with a slight eye roll from some) while waiting in line at an airport at 4 a.m.—an incredibly grand feat if I've ever seen one.

Admittedly, I initially wasn't buying into The Shane Show, but he eventually wins me over in the end. My first reaction was, *This is obnoxious, he is so loud and booming and I would like to be quiet. I would like to pretend I am not surrounded by other humans whatsoever even though we're about to sardine ourselves onto a plane. I would like to be left alone in my groggy, somewhat grumpy state. I would like to put on my noise-canceling headphones to drown out Brad and Company, thank you very much.* But even with his cheesy jokes and puns and razzing sense of humor, I am struck by the fact that Shane's demeanor was so completely *unnecessary*—it's not expected, it isn't required of him in order to fulfill the duties of his role, and yet he does it anyway. And in doing so, he completely changes the tone of the room and the otherwise tedious experience of going through security at the airport.

Shane could have done what most likely every other TSA

agent has ever done in the history of TSA agents before him: rattled off *bags and shoes in the bin; remove your laptops; all gels and liquids in a clear plastic bag; ma'am, stand here; sir, if you could wait one minute; this way; you can head over to line four; thank you,* etc., etc., in a monotone, automated voice, pointing where to stand, barely making eye contact with anyone. Shane's job is not to make us smile or to entertain us. He's there to be on the lookout for any sketchy behavior or full-size shampoo bottles, to keep the line moving, to show us where to go, and to expedite the process of making sure people aren't bringing hairspray or parakeets across the border. And hey, maybe he mostly does his shtick to keep himself entertained in a sea of zombie travelers who otherwise would look right past him. Regardless of his motivations, he goes above and beyond to be kind and bright and goofy when he doesn't need to, and his unnecessary effort is a shimmering gift to all who choose to receive it as such.

People at Dinner With Strangers often share about how disgruntled they are with the lack of connection and intention they experience within their relationships, social circles, and communities; they're unsatisfied with how little effort their friends put into making plans or how conversations with their siblings never get past the surface or how no one says hi to them at their gym. We often end up talking about where we can find spaces for connection, or how to possibly create it ourselves.

I think we forget that we can actually be agents of change in this regard, but we're looking for someone else to start the movement, to send the invitation, to be the first to ask a more vulnerable question. We are longing for connection, *and* we are longing to be *reached for,* and I think it's easier (read: less vulnerable) to write off a space or community or person as not friendly, *not our kind of place,* than to pull a Shane and take it upon ourselves to go above and beyond in the make-a-difference-to-the-people-around-us department. It makes me wonder about what it takes to shift the tide of the culture of a space—and whose responsibility it is to initiate that shift?

There are approximately nine million coffee shops within a ten-minute walk of my apartment in the west end of Toronto, and while transactionally they all provide more or less the same kind of service on the surface—varying fanciness and deliciousness of coffee, varying strength and availability of Wi-Fi, varying availability of power sockets to plug a computer into (an important factor for laptop-bearing coffee-shop-goers like me)—each coffee shop sets itself apart by the culture and social environment created by the intermingling and interaction among staff and guests. I will, without fail, always have at least some light banter, if not a good, solid chat, with any of the baristas at the narrow hole-in-the-wall coffee shop closest to my house. There's the spot on Ossington Avenue where my friend Jason always works from, always parking himself beside the chess board, willing for any patron to interrupt his workday for a game. There, people cram onto the stools in front of the espresso bar and talk about film and vinyl, and on Saturday mornings, a group of men get together to talk about vulnerability. And then there's the coffee shop one block down the street, which is the largest of the shops on the block, with floor-to-ceiling west-facing windows and light pine tables and the most space to sprawl out with a computer and notebook and the like, and not once have I been able to get past the "Hey, how's your day going?" pleasantries with any of their staff; patrons avoid eye contact with each other, even at the communal table, and the general *vibe* feels…*not* vibey. And maybe, if I'm feeling up to my *shift the culture* antics, I will comment on a book that someone brought with them that I've read or ask what the barista has going on this week, but it would take an incredible amount of investment to singularly take it upon myself to change the environment of that specific coffee shop. And I *could* invest in that! If I wanted to! I don't have to wait for permission or for someone else to initiate the change in order to be a conduit for connection wherever I am, *and* it is so beautiful to find spaces where people have collectively created a culture of connection that we get to plug ourselves into should we choose to partake.

There is an incredible opportunity as holders of spaces—whether that's the coffee shop owner or myself as an Official Dinner Host or anyone hosting a dinner gathering with their friends—to set the tone and invite people into how we want a space to feel and how we want people to engage with us and with each other there. Whether we're aware of it or not, owners / leaders / hosts / managers / Unofficial Organizer of the Group Chatters have the most influence on how people will feel within a space, and what they'll feel comfortable to do. One might say that a coffee shop owner simply wants to serve coffee and that they don't have to also create an interactive, social, communal space, and that's definitely fair; they're absolutely allowed to not put consideration and effort into building community within their space, let the coffee speak for itself, and leave it at that. And I bet it would more or less result in a transient coffee shop, one where people mostly visit because it's closest to their house or to wherever they're headed next.

I used to wrestle with how much emotional effort I was supposed to put in during my years of working in restaurants; I was an introverted artist with *so much more to me than my serving job*; I was there to be polite, considerate, attentive, and timely, make suggestions, anticipate needs, bring people their food, and, let's face it, pay my rent. What more did people want from me? A lot, sometimes. My life story, for instance, what else I did outside of work. Personality, pizzazz, a whole show of extroversion and charisma and, at times, flirting.

Throughout my twenties, I'd often treat my serving job as this massive chore and disruption to my *real work*, shifting from writing and creating and dreaming up this dinner series to putting on my all-black uniform and apron and telling every table about the pappardelle special, romancing the freshness of the calamari (*brought in fresh from the market this morning*), polishing spoons and thinking about how this was keeping me from my work that allowed me to connect with people in some meaningful way, forgetting that there were humans trying to connect—with each other, and with me—right in front of me. While there were many days I definitely didn't feel like it, existentially lamenting my

current circumstances and feeling socially taxed at work (and definitely days that I phoned it in), on the days I engaged with guests
even at a baseline level—asking what brought them in that night,
what their plans for the week were, commenting on someone's
sweater or noticing they were all in hockey jerseys and must have
been headed to the game—not only did I enjoy my shift more, but
I was often surprised by how much people would share with me,
moved to be invited into their stories, however briefly. It wasn't
exactly a part of the job description to show curiosity toward the
people I was serving, but when I did, I was almost always rewarded
with a genuine moment between a bunch of humans converging
in the strange dance of going out for dinner.

I think we actually have the ability, and even the (self-mandated)
responsibility, to shift the environment for ourselves. Want to make
gym friends? Say hi to people at the gym; compliment their bright
socks, commiserate on your mutual hate of burpees, your mutual
appreciation for when a Beyoncé song comes on, blaring for the
final five minutes of class and motivating us to get our bodies
to their best bootylicious potential. Find the artists and makers
and *doers* in your town. Show up to events, go to shows and concerts and pottery painting nights. Invite your friends, even if they
said no thanks the last three times. Invite people you *don't* know
well who you want to be your friends. Feeling like your light is
dimmed? Find the people who seem to have found the light, and

hitch your weary heart to them. Beauty and goodness and warm, open hearts are all around us.

Sometimes we have to be the first volunteers to put ourselves out there like our friend Shane at the airport, shouting puns and dad jokes out toward a line of zombie travelers in the hopes that it might make a difference to someone's day. We can, at any time, take it upon ourselves to say hi to the barista or say hi to our neighbor or engage with the boisterous group we're serving at a restaurant about their hockey jerseys as if we've never seen a boisterous group of jersey-clad humans before in our lives, just to make them feel special. We can take it upon ourselves to make goofy T-shirts for our group of friends and cheer loudly when they walk through the door even though it's early and even though it might embarrass them. I think Brad and Company would agree.

17

Dreams Don't Arrive as a Well-Thought-Out Plan; They Start as a Handful of Seeds

Bet on Yourself and Go After a Wild, Audacious Thing

After a whirlwind eight months of long-distance dating, I am shipping myself off to a new life in San Francisco to be with my boyfriend Andrew, armed with hardly anything (few belongings, barely a plan). I'm trying to become the kind of person who travels lightly, who can pick up and go, who doesn't need the sentimentality of the trinkets and treasures I've collected over the last decade. What good is a picture frame going to do? Here I am, starting over, figuratively and literally. Fresh slate. New city. New country. New life. Blank walls. Not a single throw pillow to my name.

I'm determined to find myself a Grown-Up Job: After a decade of calling myself a musician and then more vaguely an "artist," which has meant working in bars and sports arenas and private clubs and fancy restaurants and steakhouses, along with some random retail jobs scattered in between, I'm trying to become *serious.* I'm trying to star*t the rest of my life,* whatever that means. I want to be done with shift work and late nights. I'm determined to try out how the other side lives: They live nine-to-five, baby, and I want to know what that's like.

Andrew ends up pulling some strings at the start-up he works for, which I think involves at least some sweet-talking like, "Hey, will you please hire my artsy Canadian girlfriend with no professional work experience whatsoever? And don't worry, I taught her how to make a Google Calendar event last night, so she's all set."

About four days in, I know I've made a grave mistake. I can't be swayed by the impressive snack wall or free tech office lunch or even the Donut Bot the engineers made that updated a Slack channel with a live photo of the designated snack table every time someone added a treat or took one from it (okay, actually I am pretty impressed by that, but not enough to stay at a job I hate) or that everyone is very nice and I am deeply underqualified for even this entry-level role.

How could I have forgotten: I am a Creative with a handful of dreams, even if those dreams barely have any shape at this time. I am not someone motivated by consistency, stability, and predictability. That's actually the land where my motivation goes to die.

I spend an afternoon at the reception desk writing down visions and hopes and what I know to be true about myself and what I want, determined and excited to share my clarifying revelation with Andrew over dinner that night. I plan a little speech that goes something like, "Thank you so much for sweet-talking the very nice people at The Start-Up into taking a chance and giving me a job at the cool office with all the robots, but no thank you actually. I just remembered that I'm an artist and I love writing my little blog in the mornings and I have this dream of turning my weird dinner series into a business and I'm pretty sure I can make that happen, so I'll be quitting this job that you helped line up for me as I was moving across the continent and will be getting a part-time serving job where I'll make more money than at this Real Job and can meet people in the hospitality industry and get the lay of the land here."

I expect him to be thrilled by my enthusiasm and clear vision, excited to cheer me on in the direction of my (vague, mapless) dreams. Instead, he's a little…irritated. Actually, I think he's terrified. He'd signed up for the *new* version of myself that I'd presented to him, a version that I was banking on becoming in my shiny new San Francisco life, not the one I've always been—which is a woman with a bunch of seeds in my hands. "But I thought you wanted this… I thought you wanted to figure out a career," he says. And then, "I can't be with someone who is moving backward in their life." (Big ouch.) Internal alarm bells begin to sound right then and there.

We have a sobering conversation, with our different priorities, motivations, and goals starkly on display: Andrew's extremely pragmatic, ambitious demeanor clashing against my floaty, feely, artsy self. "Haven't you ever done something that made you feel really, truly, fully alive? And if not, don't you *want* to feel that way?" I ask him, thinking I am making a really compelling point, and trying to get him to catch the vision of how I am feeling.

"Sure, Jess, that would be great, but that's not how the real world works."

When I tell him I feel incredible conviction about following my heart and pursuing my dream of bringing Dinner With Strangers to San Francisco, he mostly just hears that we would have opposite schedules, and deeper than that, he's stressed out that I would be doing something high-risk, unproven, and vague. For his part, Andrew has created a finely tuned balance between his own creative endeavors and his professional life, making time for jam sessions on evenings and weekends while continuing to work in tech. He not only hopes that I'm able to find the same balance for myself but also feels like he's found the answer for me, earnestly offering the solution that's worked for him, and he's frustrated (or, more aptly, feeling helpless) that I don't seem to want what he thinks is best. He believes that, if I stick it out, I'll come to see that finding pockets of time to make art while working a corporate job will bring peace of mind and, from that, a more fulfilled life overall. While he's well-intentioned, I immediately feel like he's trying to install on me a one-size-fits-all solution instead of seeing and supporting what I believe I need to do for myself. It makes me feel like he doesn't understand me and makes me feel incredibly alone.

We go back and forth. He pleads, "It takes time to settle into a new city. You have to put in your time right now. You have to start somewhere. No one likes their first job. And you just moved here—I don't want to be passing ships in the night with opposite schedules. Can you just give this a minute?"

Since Andrew is my only anchor to San Francisco, and our relationship is the only reason I moved here, I feel like I have no choice but to stick it out at the office. I go home with a horrible feeling in my gut, like the tiniest of fractures had just chipped at the placid glass frame of our budding relationship.

Four months later, and the robotics company we work at runs out of funding, one day calling everyone in for an all-hands meeting and laying everyone off on the spot. Suddenly, Andrew and I are both unemployed. I feel unbelievably relieved, despite the fact that we'd just moved into our own apartment and have instantly become a zero-income household. I flirt with all sorts of ideas that came with being set free from this receptionist job that I hated, including going to school to become an aesthetician and applying to be a gofer at a film company; I'm all over the map with what to do next, though still too hesitant to suggest giving the dinner series a go, without the slightest clue on how to restart it in a new city.

Committed to not flipping Andrew's world upside down any further, I get connected with an HR agency that places people in administrative roles, and I have just enough experience sitting at a desk in front of a computer to sell a story that I'm eager to apply myself and learn the ins and outs of assistant work.

I end up getting hired by a bona fide tech billionaire; he's the founder of various impressive startups who is pivoting to full-time angel investing. I'm catapulted into a world of pitch meetings and calendar organization, travel research, itinerary planning and booking, conference attendee preparation, and the occasional request to drive his fancy car home from the airport for him, maybe a stop to pick up some dry cleaning on the way.

Initially, I'm relieved to feel like at the very least my job has a function—that, at the absolute minimum, my presence makes a difference beyond just being a face that greets anyone who might walk into the office: I have tasks to complete. I have places to be. I see that my role made a difference to the ecosystem of the operation of the business. Andrew is thrilled for me, optimistic that I'll find more fulfillment in this new role with more responsibility, and counting it as impressive that, with my limited experience, I've landed a job with a prestigious investor with a healthy paycheck, health insurance, and cool perks. I work hard to settle into my new role, telling myself that I was *lucky to be there.*

The job has moments of surreal opportunities and experiences. On my third day, for instance, I go to a meeting with my boss at a prestigious university where he writes a massive check to pay for biomedical research that is changing the landscape of the way they treat cancer. I sit in on meetings with San Francisco's brightest, most promising entrepreneurs, pitching their latest ideas like a company that was the "Uber of reusable diaper deliveries" and a platform where people could pay to use luxury hotel amenities without staying the night, trendy new direct-to-consumer clothing brands, and surveillance software that could detect and identify people based on how they walk (frankly terrifying, by the way). Every day is like *Shark Tank* or Oprah's gift giveaways: $10K for this start-up, $20K for that one. I'm a fly on the wall to day one of the potential Next Big Thing.

I quickly get swept up in the erratic schedule and demands of being an executive assistant to a tech billionaire. Phone buzzing at all hours. Emails starting to roll in at 5 a.m. Menial tasks seeming like a life-or-death situation. All hands on deck when a flight in Prague is rerouted, solving where he and his family might find an appropriate meal in the middle of the night in a foreign country.

I am learning what it means to be reachable at all times.

My boss's moods are also quite erratic. Like many stereotypes of highly successful people, he is extremely ambitious, a big risk-taker, driven, with bold ideas and bold actions to bring them to life. The shadow side of this is his often intense mood swings, unpredictable and extreme, expecting his chief of staff and me to be on board with whatever he's excited about that day, and often deeply overcome by a wild rage inspired by anything from a bad day in the stock market to someone being two minutes late for a Zoom meeting. My work environment and its demands are volatile, resulting in my mental health plummeting and my work-life balance being completely off-kilter.

After a year of trying to fit into this life I've constructed with Andrew, it's time to face the music: I'm miserable at work—it's toxic by any definition. I've spent the year denying what I know I want and instead trying to conform and contort into Andrew's expectations of the kind of person he thinks I should be, pursuing the priorities he thinks I should have. I feel frozen by overwhelm and disillusion, incapable of knowing even the smallest first step toward creating a better life for myself, and he internalizes my paralyzed state as a lack of motivation or an inability to take action toward changing my circumstances. He feels helpless as I continue to recoil further into myself. We're in a really bad place in our relationship; I've completely shut down emotionally, feeling discouraged, confused, and alone. Andrew is feeling unappreciated, like I'm so lost in the depths of my existential spiral that I can't emerge at any point to make him feel like a priority. I am depressed. I am certainly a drag to be around. I feel like we are at an impasse, pulled in two opposing directions. And I don't know how I could fix any of that while staying together and staying here.

I know there is one person I can call who will speak the language of possibility and shower me in gentle light, who will remind me of who I am and what I'm made of and who will know how to make a plan, even if it seems completely outlandish and ridiculous: Ryan. I call him on a rainy December morning, spilling it all, saying out loud for the first time what I've been holding in, the San Francisco fog acting like a damp hug around me, mirroring my heavy heart.

I tell him I don't want to live here anymore. I can't be with someone who isn't able to support me in pursuing the things that make me feel fulfilled. I want to quit my job, end my relationship, and move back to Toronto to figure out how to turn Dinner With Strangers into a business. I have no idea about the "how" or even the "what" exactly, but I know in my soul that I have to run toward the thing that has been calling to me. It's been a year of ignoring it, and I can no longer shut it out.

"Come home!" Ryan exclaims. "The studio is waiting for you!" His enthusiasm welcomes me and makes me feel like it's not too late and that I can surely start over again (again). We make the loosest of plans: I'll move back, relaunch the dinner, and I'll build out a calendar for the space to become a place where other creatives and makers could launch their own projects.

When I look back at that first conversation with Andrew about wanting to quit my job and figure out what my dreams were all about, I see that it was an incredibly large request for him to get on board with; I didn't have any shape of a plan, or even a definition of what I wanted to move toward. I truly only knew that I shouldn't be working this desk job, that I wanted to host Dinner With Strangers in whatever capacity I could, and that I wanted to write every day. None of that was a business plan, or even a "this is how I'll make a modicum of income" plan. At that point I'd never even ticketed the dinner. I'd hardly been paid for any writing gigs for that matter; I'd only occasionally taken some copywriting contracts here and there, and self-published a *cute* first attempt at a poetry book that was in no way putting food on the table. I wasn't giving much of a solid idea of what Andrew's future would look like with this wayward Canadian who just showed up and flipped the script a few weeks into arriving.

It feels like we were reenacting "Jack and the Beanstalk": I'd sold the family cow for these weird little beans, not even sure what they were made of, and I was asking him to trust me. An outlandish request that would make most reasonable people wary. But outlandish magic requires outlandish faith.

With every new milestone with this project since, I know that they've sprouted from the dream I held in my hands back then in San Francisco. The seeds of this dream arrived the first day that Ryan and I began discussing the idea of Dinner With Strangers. I experienced its magic at our very first dinner. I heard it calling to me when I got to San Francisco and was trying to be serious and professional. I carried it with me when I told Andrew that I wanted to quit my receptionist job and plant the seeds that I knew I had. And I believed in it enough to start over again, to leave San Francisco and return to Toronto and follow the call.

I think we think our dreams are supposed to show up like a basket of ripe, perfect plums on our kitchen table. Somewhere we started acting like we're supposed to immediately have a well-drawn-out plan of how we're going to grow this thing. Something to sink our teeth into and show that, while risky, there are steps and logistics that prove that we know what we're doing, where we're going, and how it's going to turn out. And in lieu of all that certainty and clarity, we question our dreams' validity, or our worthiness of our dreams, when they don't arrive all ripe and ready to go.

But of course everything starts as a seed, encased in nothing but potential. Everything that it will become is somehow packed inside it and is also not yet here.

It is serious work to say yes to planting something; it takes an incredible amount of audacious hope, careful nurturing, and deep faith that something might grow out of almost nothing, despite the elements, despite what is and is not within our control. It is not for the weak of heart to trade in the family cow for a couple of beans. It will often take what feels like all of your strength and all of your sanity and all of your time. It will keep it all a secret until it unfolds in real time: the success and glory and beauty of where it's heading, as well as all of the goodness along the way.

All I know is that the things that arrive to us strange and mysterious and mystical, inviting us to embark toward something that is sure to ignite our soul, are a worthwhile pursuit. And they are patient with us as we fumble and use logic and reason to argue them away. They will keep knocking, keep whispering, keep glowing to get our attention, even on the darkest of nights.

⎯⎯

Sharing my dream with Andrew and feeling like I didn't have his unwavering support has made me consider whose voice, opinion, or advice I am seeking with any given decision; just because someone has known me for a long time (and, in some cases, my whole life) doesn't mean they understand me or know what's best for me. It also makes me see that we often accidentally project what *we* need, what *we* would do in any given situation, onto each other, instead of acting as a witness to each other's revelations. It's a delicate balance to offer a mirror to our loved ones, shedding light from a different viewpoint on something they might not be considering, while still trusting that they know themselves better than anyone else.

The world needs all sorts of people, including those who assess risk and show care in the form of worry. We need people who plan extensively and survey something from all sides before jumping in. I could use a healthy dose of those types of people in my life: When I was twenty-two, I hiked five hundred miles across Spain without even glancing at a guidebook; I've made a career out of inviting complete strangers into my home for dinner without much concern for the potential dangers involved; I moved to Toronto at nineteen with no money and no plan… It's *one* way to live a life, that's for sure.

I for one am incredibly grateful for the more levelheaded people in my life who slow my roll and help me make more informed decisions and have kept me from blowing up my life (if they can intervene to offer a word of caution before I make another rash decision on my own). But if someone is brave enough to share an idea that they are excited about, let alone if that idea seems to have *sparked* something in them, ignited a part that feels big and wild and brings them out of their comfort zone, may we all commit to not immediately telling that person all the reasons why their idea is foolhardy, or all the reasons why we think it won't work.

In a world that relies on most of us becoming a cog within the machines that keep the world moving, we are fed the narrative that it is best to be efficient and productive. Step out of line, imagine a different path, defy the status quo, and we're setting ourselves up for failure and embarrassment. The many reasons why our foolhardy dream probably won't work out are rattled off like a battle cry. Just this week I had a Zoom meeting with a local founder who is doing $50 million in sales, really *scaling his business* at record heights, who told me, "Your business funnel needs a complete overhaul if you plan on making any meaningful money from what you're doing. Otherwise, what's the point?" (I ask the void: What does *meaningful money* even *mean*?!) But dreamers, makers, and doers deal in the currency of possibility; what wasn't yet here finds its way because people envision something new, daring, and hopeful and are willing to put themselves out on the proverbial limb to give it a try.

Let me be the first to say it: If a dream comes to you, the kind that makes you catch your breath and say to yourself, "What if it COULD happen?" and if you share that wild, audacious dream with the people in your life and they tell you that the thing that is sparking inside you is foolish and that you should be reasonable and to stop being ridiculous, go tell someone else. Find the person who is going to say, "I believe in you. Let's find a way."

I could tell you a hundred stories about people I love who have gone after their dreams: Annie used to own a coffee shop (this was her first dream at twenty-two; everyone thought she was crazy for that one too) and now she designs and arranges gorgeous flower arches and billowing, whimsical bouquets for weddings. Lauren woke up one day and decided she was going to start a funk band and play at weddings; four years later, she paid the whole downpayment on her house in cash from these gigs. Brian was an engineer and now he's a graphic designer, but he will tell you that at twenty-three he stumbled on a pamphlet for film school that felt like holding whatever the center of the universe is made of in his hands; he never told a soul because he knew what they would say and instead threw out the pamphlet and never thought about it again for decades. Now he's thirty-seven and his career is slowly, slowly winding toward film sets.

This isn't to say that whatever ignites you has to have something to do with your job; I can tell you about friends who have planned wild yearlong sojourns, or for whom it felt overwhelmingly daring to simply move out of their hometown. A friend recently signed up for hip-hop classes on Wednesday nights and feels silly and awkward and loves every minute of it. Online dating might be the next great frontier for you, or therapy, or pottery class. All of it is worth pursuing if it sets your heart on fire.

My hope is that each of us finds someone in our lives that we can call when we want to talk about our unreasonable dreams. That we may say the audacious thing out loud. Lay out the outrageous plan, the map we sketched in pencil, the scribbled notes, the buried handwriting, every half-baked detail, the thing we think about in the company of our mind when we're brushing our teeth, or when we're at our job that is going well and we should be so grateful that we're employed, or around the table that we should be so thankful we're sitting at. Spare nothing when laying out your dreams. Someone will want to hear it all.

There are people in our lives who we call when we need to be brought down to earth, who will ask us to consider the facts, survey our options, and weigh the consequences. We need people who speak with a voice of reason, and we *also* need people who will mostly always tell us to go for it, whatever "it" is. These people are not the type to tell us that everyone has to do things they don't like. They aren't quick to point out that we may end up looking like a fool. They are the people who know that there are all different kinds of risks and ramifications, including the ones that come with ignoring the dreams we have that make our entire being feel electric and the ones that smother the spark that feels like our life force.

My hope is that we open ourselves up to be worthy witnesses of each other's dreams. May we be quick to believe in the possibility of anything daring, wild, and electric. May we be brave enough to pay attention to what sets our hearts on fire, and brave enough to go after it.

18

In Defense of Just Going for It
Find the Resolve to Take the Leap

Ryan and I, both visionaries and dreamers who tend to egg each other into the farthest-reaching stratosphere of possibility (as in: not being particularly skilled at execution of tasks and instead being generally *reasonable* about plans), took nearly six months to solidify our first dinner after the idea first came to us. We overthought and overplanned. We talked in circles and shot for the moon and came back down again. We made a list of every single person we knew who might want to come and strategized who should be at which dinner together. We'd get sidetracked, spending hours talking about how to make the dinner a podcast before we had even hosted a single dinner, and then another night wondering if it could be a show without either of us being in front of a video camera a day in our lives. We'd conceptualize and dream and second-guess and go back to the drawing board over and over again. Based on our skill sets and temperaments, we're an unlikely duo to have gotten this project off the ground from an organizational standpoint, but Ryan is the kind of person you want along for any kind of ride if you can pin him down.

When we started conceptualizing Dinner With Strangers, we'd get together for "meetings," which mostly involved getting lunch and fighting over who paid and maybe splitting a bottle of wine and theorizing on how the dinner would go. We'd get stumped on how to prepare dinner for ten people when we could barely cook for ourselves (we live, after all, in the epicenter of culinary excellence that is Toronto, so why would *we* ever need to master the art of making a large meal, especially when hosting said meal in a lower-level hair studio / flower studio that has a kitchenette and no oven?). "Let's think on it," we'd say, and a few weeks would go by, and we'd meet again, get all excited, spitball some ideas, and then think some more.

One day during one of our "meetings," I finally said, "You know what, Ry, I think we should just put a date in the calendar, invite some people, and see what happens. No matter how much we prepare, there are some things we're just not going to know until we try this." We randomly selected a midweek night in May and hosted our first Dinner With Strangers gathering.

On event day, we met at 11 a.m., bought enough food for lunch and dinner for thirty people (even though there would be eight people joining Ryan and me for dinner), made homemade salad dressings and slow-roasted chickpeas and chopped veggies and had our inaugural now-long-standing tradition of a *porch beer,* which is less specific to the location (on a porch or not on a porch) or the kind of beverage you drink (beer or not beer) but became the moniker for the drink break at around 4 p.m., when all the prep is done and everything's cooking and you've done all you can until you need to do all the last-minute tasks right before guests arrive, like lighting the candles and setting up the drinks station with ice and having a momentary freak-out about the fact that a bunch of strangers are about to descend upon your studio in the hopes that something great is going to happen.

We overprepared our questions. We spent forever overthinking where everyone would sit. We were a little flustered and nervous ten minutes before everyone was set to show up, a shared *what are we about to do and is this going to be a disaster?* glance between us. Our beautiful friends who didn't know each other showed up for our weird social experiment, and it was the most incredible evening. It was the beginning of something magical. When every dish was washed and the studio was put back to its usual state, I floated home on a cloud.

I learn something new about facilitating every time I host an event: a new icebreaker question that doesn't feel forced. A more seamless way to transition from side chatter to a collective conversation. What to prepare ahead of time so I'm not figuring it out in the moment. How to automate emails. Admitting that I need a proofreader for typos and someone to double-check that Friday is December 6, not December 1, and that the invitation reflects the correct date and that time zones are included in online invites (Lord Jesus, deliver me from the administrative tasks that I cannot execute correctly. Actually, deliver me from all administrative tasks, amen). I get better at this work every time, and there is still so much to learn. And I promise you, if I didn't force myself to just try to see what happens, I'd still be standing at the drawing board, trying to figure out where and when to start.

If you have a dream that is floating around inside you, don't wait until you think you know what you're doing before you start doing the thing you're thinking about doing. Prepare, yes. Do your research. Get the appropriate training and mentorship if your dream requires it. Immerse yourself in the world of the dream. Look up who else is in a similar arena as you and see where and how they got started; map out the plot points of their success trajectory if you can. Plan, plan, plan. Make an outline and a road map and have at least a few contingencies. Ask for advice. Bounce ideas off friends. And then: Get going. Begin. Try. And then try again.

———

Caleb, a local poet, asks if we can meet for coffee so he can pick my brain about artist stuff and hosting stuff. We meet on a rainy fall day, and he tells me about his work, how he wants to create art that makes people feel less lonely, and how he wants to host live events that give people the space to talk about heartbreak. He hosted a gathering at a local bar last spring, and despite his large social media following, he was disappointed with the low attendance. He took the poor turnout as a sign that hosting these live events isn't worth it, or that they're not what people want, or maybe even that people don't want to go to something that *he's* hosting. He leapt right to the conclusion that it was a personal rejection of himself and his work because only a few people bought tickets.

I, too, have been quick to jump to conclusions and, even deeper than that, to tie a less than ideal outcome to rejection of the work, when so much of this is just reasonable, boring, objective business-y stuff like understanding the demographics of his audience (while he has a strong online following, are they local to where he lives? Are they underage and therefore couldn't attend because it was in a bar?), examining how his event was marketed (was it clear what the event entailed? Should he have posted about it more frequently? Did he sell tickets in order to have a better gauge of interest and the amount of marketing push he needs to put behind it to fill the room? Should he start an email list specifically for people who are interested in live events? Could he collaborate with another artist in order to share the workload of promoting a live event?), and getting more feedback from his online audience about what kind of live events they'd be interested in attending (while his audience may love how open and vulnerable he is in his poetry about heart-ache, maybe they're not ready to publicly share about their own, and hosting a poetry reading rather than an interactive event would have been less intimidating for them).

I share all this with Caleb, and then I encourage him to try again after reflecting on these considerations. Determining that the whole concept for the event will never work based on one event's low attendance is simply not enough data to arrive at that conclusion. I say this as a highly sensitive artist who feels like everything I put out there is incredibly personal (because it is); tickets for an event go live, and I'm glued to my inbox, thinking, *Hi. I put this thing I love out into the universe. Do you love it?* So slow ticket sales or low turnout or the fact a poem that I poured my entire soul into didn't go viral on Instagram feels like a direct rejection of ME, instead of all the many other explanations for why those things can happen.

Taking action, opting in, saying yes, committing to something: These are the attributes that matter most. Much more than talent, resources, or experience. Those come with time. In a world where most people are afraid to look silly, to fail spectacularly, to put themselves out there and put their names behind something that might not work, those who are willing to simply begin and see where it takes them are vastly ahead of the game.

Call it a *Test Run*. Call it a *Pilot*. Call it a *Dress Rehearsal*. Give it a name that feels exploratory if that feels safer. Remember that this whole business of chasing your dreams is supposed to be fun (or fulfilling or meaningful or or or).

The world is waiting for the magic that is already alive within you.

19

On Apocalypse, and the Ways We've Already Figured Out How to Survive

We Each Have Something to Contribute to Our Communities

Growing up, I always secretly kind of fancied myself the heroine in a hypothetical dystopian postapocalyptic storyline. I would be, maybe, the chosen one (would I feign hesitancy or reluctance? That really does something for the plot, you know) to rally the group, give some inspired speech, lead us into battle against whatever it was we were fighting. Maybe I'd be invited to be, like, I don't know, a thought leader for the new way of governance, touting *everybody just take a breath,* touting *what would Mary Oliver have to say about this?,* touting great and impressive questions like *how can we best take care of each other so that no one is left behind?* (I will tell you right now, I will not be brought in for snappy decision-making, operations, implementation, or anything practical. If I'm the best person for the job, wow, our new world is going to be teetery on the rollout of these new Ways of Living.)

I, like approximately 99 percent of North America, was swept up in the hype of the critically acclaimed show *The Last of Us* as soon as it came out. For those of you who haven't indulged in the cultural phenomenon that is Pedro Pascal's furrowed brow, Bella Ramsey's spitfire what-are-they-going-to-do-next attitude, and Nick Offerman's singular performance as an absolutely charming doomsday prepper who will make you cry every time you see a strawberry for the rest of your life, *The Last of Us* is a show (based on a video game) about a postapocalyptic world that takes place after a mutated fungus kills nearly everyone. There are only a marginal number of zombielike fungus-monsters involved (i.e., tolerable for the squirmy and jump-scare averse).

I think it's pretty much the first intense—certainly the first dystopian—show I've consumed since the pandemic changed our world (during and since which I've pretty strictly kept myself exclusively watching *RuPaul's Drag Race*; I've had no capacity to take in anything remotely dramatic / dystopian / high-stakes of any kind), and it had me reconsidering my opinion of Hypothetical Apocalyptic Jess, what role I can picture for myself, and whether I would want to stick around, insist on, and help create a safe, beautiful new reality for humankind.

Who am I, really, to shank a zombielike fungus-monster between the eyes with a dull steak knife while running for my life? Do I really want to spend decades in a quarantine zone on food stamps, trading—what, poems? LOL—on the black market for a can of chickpeas? And this is to say nothing about a world without coffee beans and deodorant. I am (perhaps, probably) too fickle to live without them. Maybe I'd give it a week and then send myself out to pasture. Bye-bye.

I've been sitting with this a lot: the idea of giving up the fight. Or not being interested in getting in there in the first place.

And then I started thinking: The world has already ended a thousand times and continues to end all over the place. It has ended, over and over again. It's ended in Syria, in Germany. It's ended during the Troubles in Ireland, bombed-out schools and grocery stores and every church for miles. It ends every day when people have to give up their homes because of medical debt, when people can't get access to food, water, medical aid, when people have to shit on the street because they could get arrested in a Starbucks if they don't buy a latte first (it ends every day that people's only option for an accessible bathroom is a Starbucks). The world has ended and continues to end in Afghanistan, in Iran. It ends right here where I can't bring myself to have a coffee with an old friend because our differing political views feel like an insurmountable divide. It ends every time someone says, *yeah, but what can we even do,* or *nothing will ever change,* or *my vote doesn't matter,* or *everything is corrupt, so why try,* or *I wish I could go back to the good old days.*

In every one of these instances of the world ending, people have stayed. People have said, *not so, I won't have it.* Have said, *here is a better way.* People have fallen in love in Ireland, in Afghanistan, have written songs and played them for each other, have made up games for kids huddling in bomb shelters, have played cards while sitting on the sidewalk, have found ways to write letters, make secret codes, feed each other, share what they have.

At Dinner With Strangers, we often share about turning points and fresh starts. People talk about leaving the countries they were born in, leaving small towns or bustling cities, pivoting mid-university to take up a completely different degree in a different state. They tell stories about painful family dynamics, grief and death and disappointment. With increasing regularity, we shake our heads at *the state of things,* wondering what's to be done, what's coming next, what the world will look like even a year from now. When we look back on these stories of our origin and history, we are reminded that we've been through so much, born from generations of people who went through so much. We have found a way to survive.

I don't need to ask myself who I would be in an apocalypse situation. We are in one, have been in one, just like the many who have come before us. The unveiling of this time and the ways I respond are who I am. (Is this too ridiculous to ask myself if I care to be a part of the revolution?)

Last fall I was talking with a family member about the latest whatever-it-was that felt like the end of the world (probably another school shooting), and she said to me, "This is how God makes us ready for heaven—the turmoil, the guns, the hatred. I can't take it anymore. I'm ready to go anytime." It made me upset on multiple levels—that she would be so ready to leave this earth and, by doing so, leave me. And I also felt protective of this world, this world I work so hard to love, this world I work so hard to find all that is redeemable and good about, despite. I work so hard to insist that this life and this world are worth the fuss.

The world begins again every time we open a door for a stranger. Every time we teach a kid about accepting each other for who we are. Every time we get out of bed. Every time we say *enough* and insist that things can be different. Every time we call a friend. Every time we look for the helpers and help them help. Every time we slow our pace down enough to pay attention. Every time we can't sleep and get up and write down everything that hurts until we find the right word for the thing. Every time we do say something to someone that our younger selves needed to hear. Every time we ask a teenager what they think. Every time we share someone's art. Every time we say *I'm sorry.* Every time we say *I forgive you.* Every time we say *let's try again.*

20

Empirical Evidence That People Are Good

Let the Goodness of Others Give You Strength

This morning I am stopped in my tracks by an image we've seen far too much in the last ten months: A wailing mother is bent over her son who was killed wailing. She kisses his hands, his face, cradles him in the way you would cradle your own heart outside of your body. She and I don't speak the same language and yet she is speaking the language that we all speak when we are in anguish.

At a Dinner With Strangers in Brooklyn, I ask the group, "What is something you used to believe but don't anymore?" and Elias shares, "I used to believe that humans are mostly good—generally good—that at our core, there is goodness there. And now I don't know if I don't believe that anymore." His double-negative way of phrasing this is accompanied by a gentle, forlorn smirk. We all sigh. We all nod. We scrunch our lips in the way people do when they don't want to agree with what was said, but don't know how to *not* agree. I think for a minute and then say, "I have the ability to offer some optimism because of the unofficial statistical data I'm gathering with these dinners. May I offer some of that optimism in rebuttal?"

At the dinner table, with wild regularity, I am confronted with the stories of people doing their best. I get to bear witness to people surviving things like hungry childhoods and angry fathers and parents who didn't understand them and homophobic slurs slung at them at school every day for four years and then witness those people coming out on the other side with so much gentleness in their eyes it could make your knees turn to goo.

On Wednesday, just this week, a woman tells us about the day she left her husband. He told her for the four-hundred-millionth time that her work was meaningless and her business name was stupid and no one would want a fifty-seven-year-old personal trainer and no one would ever be attracted to a woman with so much muscle (himself included, himself specifically). In response, and by response I mean defiance, she made T-shirts and ball caps and tote bags that said STRONG in a big, swirly typeface that she chose with care, putting this word that encapsulated so much more to her than a statement about a workout on clothes that she put up for sale on her online store, and she sold out of her merch in minutes. Two years later, she now lifts massive plates over her head with precision and badassery. She teaches other women how to do the same (both the lifting and the leaving).

I hear stories about the people who've made all the difference in people's lives: coaches who saw something special and were sure to call it out and social workers at middle schools who got them signed up for extracurriculars. I hear about older brothers who always made them feel included and uncles who were the only people to make sure they said, "Just so you know, I will always love you, no matter what, exactly as you are," when they came from a family that would not, in fact, love them no matter what, specifically if they chose to love the person they loved out loud.

I sit at the table with normal people who come from somewhere, maybe here, maybe an unthinkable childhood, maybe a lonely life or a self-proclaimed blessed life, who are doing the same thing I am: trying to listen, trying to make some meaning, trying to find a thread of beauty or hope in this dumpster fire of a world, trying to see what is in their power to make a difference. We are looking for all the ways we can do our part.

If I were to act like a scientist and gather all this data, which in soul language we might call *proof,* and put it on some sort of graph, I would see a line emerge in the shape of an arrow going forward toward the light.

———

The other day I passed a man who was yelling, as people are wont to do; he was shouting various grievances and various profanities to no one, which is to say anyone, which is to say anyone who'd listen, which is to say anyone in his general vicinity who couldn't help but hear. *This city,* he yelled, and *these people* and *nobody cares* and *nobody sees* and *this place is going to shit* and [profanity profanity] and *no one says hi to anyone anymore in this goddamn place.*

Just as our proclaiming man says this last sentiment, another voice enters the rhetorical chat: "Hey, brother!" a friendly stranger says in response, interrupting his declarations and proving his sentiment incorrect. "How's it going?" The proclaiming man is startled. *Oh!* he says. Someone has, in fact, said hello. And says something else. I'm too far away to hear what happens after that. I like to think they chatted at least briefly, sharing in the human experience of meeting each other exactly where they're at.

It got me thinking about the conclusions we all come to about this world: that it is anything but kind, that we are powerless, that nothing changes and nothing will change, that people don't say hello, which is proof that no one cares, which is proof of everything else wrong with people these days. We might be proven wrong in our hopelessness by one gentle gesture from a stranger who is willing to say hi, which could happen at any time.

This is a world of our own making: the madness, the cruelty, the apathy, and also this—that a man might, in his anger, declare that he feels unseen, and someone else will stop what they're doing to make sure he knows he's not alone in this horrible, wonderful city, in this godforsaken earth filled with people on the lookout, vigilantly, for ways they can take care of each other.

I refuse to believe that we don't care about each other. I have been a witness to too much care to be able to be convinced otherwise. We take care of the people in our immediate circle and also strangers, also neighbors, also people scattered across the world. We make grand gestures of care and also show the simplest of care right here at the table by listening to each other's stories and holding out a napkin when eyes get misty and affirming when something resonates and asking how else we can show up for one another.

I refuse to believe that we aren't collectively able to imagine, create, and demand a better world and a better way. We have been doing that since the beginning, since the day the word *enough* was invented. And we can claim enough is enough at any time. Like right now, even. I write it down so many times it doesn't even look like a word anymore. Enough. Enough. Enough.

21

This Could Happen Anywhere

Letting These Lessons Alter Your Everyday Life

I'm a few months into relaunching Dinner With Strangers, and I'm feeling a bit overwhelmed; this project feels like it was skyrocketing in a way I couldn't have predicted, and making sure to deliver a meaningful, welcoming, dare I even say FUN event takes care and a hell of a lot of elbow grease. People are buying tickets and showing up and trusting me to lead these conversations, and they were willing to share their stories with each other. I have what many would call a *business* on my hands, all while figuring out how to create an email list and learn how to market myself and send timely, informative emails, hopefully without typos. My bones are tired and my soul is so, so full.

It's my fifth dinner at Roof Garden, and our conversation is focused on the theme "Traditions & Rituals." To begin, everyone shares their favorite tradition: Some center on various holidays; someone shares about their annual walk they take on May 9, commemorating a specific turning point in their life; someone shares how much they loved going to Staples for back-to-school shopping when they were a kid, and now they make sure to make it a Big Deal when they take their partner's kids shopping for school supplies at the end of the summer each year. My cheeks quickly hurt from smiling—it's beautiful to hear a room of people talk about the things they decide to put emphasis on, the things we do to mark important days or important people in our lives.

Our main discussion is about things we used to believe but don't anymore—like believing that life is fair and life is long and that high school grades could impact our entire future and that being an adult would be fun and that what we are able to afford might bring us fulfillment—and I was struck by our ability to change, our ability to unlearn what was taught to us, our ability to change our minds given the evidence around us.

It's such an inspiring and uplifting night, and at the end, someone comments, "Jess, this is an amazing thing you're doing because this truly doesn't happen anywhere." Since I'm the person running this thing, that's probably a good sign that he thinks that; marketing folks would say I'm *fulfilling a need*, right? Something about *supply and demand*, something about *scarcity*, something about *addressing a pain point in the market*. And to an extent, I get what they're saying; Dinner With Strangers was inspired by wanting to create a space for the types of connection and conversation that I love to have, that don't happen everywhere. I wanted to make this weird social experiment come to life and see where it goes. And I've seen the wild response to this project as confirmation that we are looking for ways to connect with each other; we are innately wired for connection and don't always know how to get there; we are looking to feel inspired and learn from each other and find places to share from our hearts. And it's really incredible that people have seen this project and said, "YES! THAT! I'm in!"

And also.

Connection is available to us at any time. It's right there for the taking all over the place: with our neighbors and with the person who goes to the gym at the same time as us and with our coworkers and our hairdresser / barista / bookshop owner / Uber driver. We can marvel at the unseasonably warm weather. We can compliment their scarf. We can ask them what they're excited about lately. We can ask them what they love about hair / coffee / books / driving strangers around. We can ask them what brought them here. We can ask about their day. We can ask them anything that shows that we're interested and shows presence and shows that we are reaching for them.

It's a mix of busyness and social decorum and maybe some overthinking about how it might be received by the other person that often keeps us from crossing these borders between anonymity and familiarity, between casual interaction and any amount of vulnerability on any given day.

I always think about how we pretend our lives aren't all interconnected and overlapping when I'm taking public transit; our bodies press together in a way we'd like to pretend they don't in the same way we try to pretend our lives aren't the same as anyone else's here. We are close, so we are uncomfortable—our knees knock together and we are a tangle of arms reaching for something on which to anchor our hands. The server running late for their lunch shift impatiently taps their foot that is swinging into the middle of the aisle. The mother with three tiny backpacks strung along her arms wrangles three small bodies into seats. The businessperson and the barista are getting off at the same block to work at their very different jobs in the same tall building; the shift workers and the artists have the same music pulsing through their noise-canceling headphones. We drown out the sounds of our closeness with podcasts and playlists.

This morning while I'm waiting for the streetcar to arrive, a woman using a paper face mask as a headband asks me for a cigarette. I find myself wishing I smoked just so I'd have something tangible to offer her. A man boards the trolley at the same time as me holding a massive bouquet of yellow flowers, and I wonder where he's taking them at 8:34 a.m. Halfway through my trip, a man is saying his morning prayers to himself (and presumably to God, I suppose), and the man sitting beside him says, "*I don't know how prayer works, man. My son died a year ago. That's my story. That's where I'm coming from"*—grief so cavernous he can't not say it to a stranger praying beside him. Bare as anything could be, his whole story placed out in the open for all of us to hear. What a wild convergence: one man trying to connect with God on a streetcar, one man trying to connect with anyone who will look him and his grief in the eye.

I press the button to let the driver know this is my stop and walk down my street, past the houses that house my neighbors, all separate from each other, held apart by walls and bricks and windows and the decorum of pretending none of this is intertwined or the same in any way.

———

I recognize that it's unrealistic to live with a constant awareness and attunement to the opportunities for deep, meaningful connection; we have places to be and lists to complete, and truly, constantly addressing the marvel and mystery and tragedy and interconnectedness of the world simply is too much to face at every minute of the day. We'd never get anything done. Maybe our brains would quite literally explode; who's to say. But I wonder what it would look like if we each dialed up our awareness for these opportunities to be present to the people around us, strangers and loved ones alike, maybe by 10 percent? If we could slow down enough and were aware enough to pull back from our own to-dos and what's-nexts, how much would that change how connected we feel to others?

We get to, at any time, when we have the capacity, when we're able to look up, when we're able to catch the moment, open ourselves up to each other. There are a million invitations every day. And not everyone is going to catch on to our outstretched hands. We all know what it's like to be busy and distracted and, hell, me of anyone, lost in the abyss of my inner world while also being en route to buy olive oil.

We are disconnected and simulating intimacy with likes and shout-outs and tags; we get swept up and distracted by senseless arguments in the comments section and posturing and pretending we have it all together and networking and hacking away and capitalism and brokenheartedness and our side and their side and silos of thought and cancel culture and all the other things that make us weary and make us wary of someone approaching us just to chat. But we need to find a way out of this disconnection. We need Big Change. We need an apocalypse of priorities and The Way Things Have Been.

People often write to me and share that they're incredibly inspired by Dinner With Strangers and feel this fire within them to start their own dinner or event or series or gathering that will have a similar effect, and they're not sure where to start. And while I'm incredibly proud of this project and know that there's something really special about an immersive, intentional night with a specific mission to get past small talk and share our stories, I don't think anyone needs to wait for these "official" or "curated" spaces of connection in order to find meaningful connection right where we're at. We can start now. We can start here. We can start with messaging someone at any time and letting them know we're thinking of them. Maybe, maybe, we could even ask when they're free for a coffee. We can be on the lookout for one stranger a week to interact with. We can ask our families one good question at family gatherings that get people talking about how they're actually doing rather than just shooting the shit over mashed potatoes.

We have so far to go, and we can start anytime. How daunting. How simple. Let's go together.

What My Bio Doesn't Say

Jess Janz is a wild bundle of sensitive feelings. She is mostly an ocean, a storm, anything that crashes, not necessarily as in *loud* but as in *so much, all at once.* Born with an angst pinned to the inside of her throat, her first words were probably *how does it feel?* and she is probably looking for the right time to ask you at some point. She grew up on the rainy coast that borders the edge of anything precise and still forgets to bring an umbrella.

Jess has written some things but is unsure if she should list any of them. She read somewhere that she should list all of them. She is aware that this bio is supposed to be an attempt to come off as impressive. She considers telling you about the time she drove a dinosaur tooth to Berkeley. She considers telling you everything she's thought since breakfast. She thinks she could say more. She wonders if she should say less. Jess is usually worried she's gone on too long and should go find somewhere to sit instead.

Jess has made a life out of chasing stillness down like an animal sprinting toward the sun in the tall grass. She has made a life out of quiet mornings. She has made a life out of long phone calls while on an afternoon walk. She is making a life out of listing all the different words for longing. She is making a life out of holding hands.

She now resides in that place between maybe taking it all a little too seriously and forgetting to pick up olive oil on her way home.

She lives with her own company and her worry, for whom she is learning to make a soft bed.

Acknowledgments

Writing is a solitary practice, but bringing this book into the world was possible only because I've been encircled by the care, wisdom, and encouragement of so many:

Ryan Cantelon dreamed up Dinner With Strangers with me, brought it to life, and infused it with magic. He is a beacon of optimism and possibility to everyone he encounters, inspiring loved ones and strangers alike to sprint toward whatever sets their hearts on fire;

Jonathan Merritt saw something in my work before I saw it myself and was the first to bet on me as an author. He fostered no fewer than three (!!!) book proposals with me as my fearless and persistent literary agent, and he's my favorite person with whom to banter about a celebrity (or real-life) crush;

Ariel Curry edited this manuscript with thoughtfulness and

enthusiasm, weathering my doubts with focused guidance and bringing clarity, shape, and meaning to the book;

Brian Kall read the earliest batch of essays and talked through the concept, message, and mission of many chapters. He said exactly what I needed to hear to cast my doubts aside and get back to the page;

Jason Zerbin shouldered the bulk of my artist spirals throughout the writing process, offered insight and creativity to get me unstuck, and created space for brainstorming, venting, second-guessing, and weathering (a few) pity parties as the fickle, feely artist that I am;

Alyssa Rittenberg, Annalise Parady, Candace Kronen, Cassie Connor, Elizabeth Reynolds Lopushinsky, Jon Peck, Jessica Schafer, Misha Glouberman, Nicole Antonacci, Nicole Jasper-Lawless, Sam Bradshaw, Sasha Vazquez, Taniya Gupta, and Tristan Richards were early readers of this project and offered wisdom and insight that truly made this book better;

Lauren Bramlett combed through my neurosis and overthinking, editing multiple chapters with extra care, helping me to see the through-threads and clarify language and message;

Cassie Connor talked through my stickiest chapters and has held many tender things along with me over the years;

Toussaint Morrison offered wise insight and was a vital sounding board for this project;

Joél Leon sent many a voice note pep talk and graciously let me tease out core ideas, themes, and messages;

Amanda Smith has held the door open for me in countless

literal and metaphorical ways. I've hosted multiple dinners, wrote my book proposal, and finished the first draft of this book at her Vancouver apartment, and she's been a mentor, adviser, style icon, and dear friend for decades;

Petrina Pecknold handed me the keys to her apartment for a week of silence and solace that made way for so many of these pages. Your Joy is infused into this book;

Lance Odegard has been a mentor, coach, thinking partner, and dear adviser as I've navigated this work as a facilitator and accidental entrepreneur;

Lavanya Lakshmi offered insight and camaraderie continuously throughout the publishing process. She was the first to give me permission to be excited about this book deal and met for a particularly vital emergency Aperol spritz and literal hand-holding when I needed it most;

Jennifer Nickle leads with her whole heart, which she puts into every menu she designs and dish she prepares, which have been at the center of so many dinners. She's navigated the wildness of the last two years as a fiercely loyal friend and copilot;

Nat and Phil Caravaggio have been an integral part of the success of Dinner With Strangers, giving this project a fresh start with plenty of space to grow at Roof Garden;

Estefania Ochoa is everything professional, beautiful, cool, and good about the With Strangers brand, which has contributed to the success of my business and this project in innumerable ways;

Adam Deunk came out of photography retirement to take my

author photo and universally makes everyone he's around feel like the shiniest, glowyest versions of themselves, not just when we're trying to look professional and glamorous for the camera;

Maiya Chan took the cover photo for this book at a dinner in 2023, and she perfectly captured the messy, beautiful dance of communing with each other; Philip Atkins and Christopher Favale have enveloped me like a fifth sister, offering a lifetime of insight and encouragement and extending their table for multiple dinners in Brooklyn;

KP taught me the necessity of burying our dreams like a seed (or a mint tin);

Matthew Lindholm knows the ins and outs of every fear, heartache, doubt, dream, triumph, mistake, good date, bad date, lesson, and opportunity that has crossed my path. He's been here for the biggest and the most trivial things and makes me feel at home in my wild, swirling heart;

My parents, Rod and Kath, have always fervently pointed me in the direction of my dreams, insisting that I continue to pursue my creative work even when (especially when) it hasn't made sense. They are the force that settles and sends me;

And one thousand one hundred and seven strangers have sat at tables with me across the continent over the last nine years, sharing their stories, thoughts, and lessons that have shaped who I am and inspired every word of this book;

For these tangible contributions and for every invisible, immeasurable offering in between, I am forever grateful. Thank you.

About the Author

© Adam Deunk

Jess Janz is a writer, community facilitator, and the creator of *Dinner With Strangers*, a project devoted to bringing people together through thoughtfully designed conversations. She's mostly asking questions and telling stories about identity, connection, and what binds us all together. She comes from the West Coast and is currently living in Toronto.